WITHDRAWAL

From

RESEARCH

American Enterprise Institute
Studies in Health Policy

Marion Ein Lewin,
editor

into POLICY

*Improving the Link for
Health Services*

From Research into Policy

From Research into Policy

Improving the Link for Health Services

Marion Ein Lewin, editor

American Enterprise Institute for Public Policy Research
Washington, D.C.

I thank the Pew Memorial Trust for its support of the seminars and research that made this book possible. I would also like to extend my appreciation to Lynn L. Lewis for her substantive review of the papers and helpful suggestions and to Melinda Kicherer for her administrative assistance.

R A   M.E.L.
3 9 4
.F 7 6
1 9 8 6

Library of Congress Cataloging-in-Publication Data

From research into policy.

Bibliography: p.
1. Medical policy—United States.
2. Medical care—Research—United States.
3. Medical care—Cost control—Research—
United States.   I. Lewin, Marion Ein.
II. American Enterprise Institute for Public
Policy Research.   [DNLM: 1. Health Services
Research—United States.   2. Policy Making.
W   84.3   F931]
RA394.F76   1986   362.1'0973   86-14129
ISBN 0-8447-3605-8

1 3 5 7 9 10 8 6 4 2 December 19, 1989

AEI Studies 445

Printed in the United States of America

Contents

President's Foreword

The chapters in this volume, commissioned under a grant to AEI from the Pew Memorial Trust, focus on a theme of great interest and importance to decision makers in the world of health care: the role of health services research in the formulation of policies and programs. These four case studies examine major federal and state initiatives in the areas of containing health care costs, developing prospective payment/diagnosis-related groups (DRGs) for hospitals, improving access to maternal and child health services, and reforming nursing home reimbursement. They look at the contribution of health services research to shaping those efforts.

Three years ago the Pew Memorial Trust launched the Pew Health Policy Program, a continuing program of which AEI is a part, to provide current and potential leaders in health care decision making with specialized postgraduate training and an opportunity to expand their knowledge of relevant policy concerns and the policy process. Several leading institutions across the country were chosen to develop special programs in health: Boston University and Brandeis University; the University of California at San Francisco; the University of Michigan; and the Rand Corporation and the University of California at Los Angeles.

A fifth grant was awarded to AEI's Center for Health Policy Research to conduct two major conferences each year for the fellows and faculty participating in the program. The essays, written on timely topics, serve as background papers for discussion at the conferences and are also published for wider dissemination. AEI is particularly pleased to be a part of the Pew Health Policy Program because of our own research efforts in studying new directions in health policy and disseminating the results of our investigations, site visits, and convening activities throughout the public and private sectors.

From Research into Policy: Improving the Link for Health Services is the third in a series of publications based on scholarly papers produced for the Pew Health Policy Program. The first two books in this series are *The Health Policy Agenda: Some Critical Questions*, edited by Marion

Ein Lewin, acting director of the Center for Health Policy Research, and *Incentives vs. Controls in Health Policy: Broadening the Debate*, edited by Jack A. Meyer, AEI resident fellow in economics and former director of the center.

PAUL W. MCCRACKEN
President
American Enterprise Institute

Foreword

It is almost fifteen years since a report by President Nixon's Science Advisory Committee highlighted the need for a broader understanding and appreciation of research and development as a means of improving health care in the United States.[1] It concluded that "government must have the capacity to anticipate problems in the provision of health services, to formulate coherent and coordinated policies and standards for our pluralistic health care system, and to stimulate the development, testing, and evaluation of new forms of organization and technology that will improve the health care system." In the opinion of the committee, "success in these endeavors depends to a great extent on the relatively new field of health services R & D."

At the time of the report's publication, many policy makers were doubtful that health services research could play any significant role in improving medical care in this country. This group held that the nation's health care arrangements were shaped by professional tradition, economic circumstances, and political conditions and that research results could not be expected to alter this situation.

Many in the scientific community were similarly doubtful. They felt that health-policy-oriented research would not be able to gain scientific acceptance within academic medicine, nursing, economics, sociology, and other relevant disciplines. In addition, serious questions were raised about the ability of this new field to recruit and train skilled young scientists, to develop sophisticated research methods, to gain access to the major scientific journals, or to garner support for new research centers within major universities or existing policy institutes.

Yet, surprisingly, a decade and a half later both these concerns have been put to rest. Research on the efficacy of health maintenance organizations (HMOs), diagnosis-related groups (DRGs), state hospital rate setting, small area variations in the use of medical and hospital care, the efficiencies of for-profit hospitals, and the Rand health insurance experiment and a myriad of other health policy studies have shown that research results can lead to changes in America's health care system.

Likewise, recent years have seen scientific recognition of this field by most of the relevant professions, journals, university disciplines, and professional schools and by a range of public and private funding agencies. The issue of whether health policy research is a legitimate field of scientific inquiry within universities and established policy institutes has been settled. It is.

Today the concerns of the health policy research community are of another dimension. How can this applied field better disseminate its findings so that necessary improvements in the nation's health care system occur more swiftly? To address this question effectively requires thinking about health services research somewhat otherwise than in earlier years. At the time of the President's Science Advisory Committee report, it was thought that health services research was analogous in its development and use to biomedical science. But in reality a better analogy for health policy research is what many universities call an "area study." The idea for area studies programs in universities arose during World War II in an attempt to focus individual university disciplines on the broad problems of winning the war in the Pacific and on our nettlesome relations with our Russian allies. The object was to get experts from many fields working together on one particular problem like the war effort or diplomatic issues that would subsequently emerge. In more recent years the area study model has been adapted to domestic problems, particularly in urban and environmental studies and, more recently, in health care.

In U.S. programs of urban studies, environmental studies, Asian studies, and health policy research, what I would call "an iron law of area studies" exists. It has a number of tenets, one of the most important of which is this: "Experts," not research, bring about change. This tenet is of particular relevance for today's concerns. Medicine is almost unique in the United States in that its key decision makers are both knowledgeable about research and often the leading practitioners in the major university hospitals in the nation's largest communities. These physician leaders generally read published research studies and, if they find something new, dramatic, or interesting, present it to their house staff, fellows, and practicing physicians at the hospital. Often this leads to the incorporation of new innovations into clinical practices. The same academic physicians are often likely to offer huge continuing education programs for practicing physicians within their community, state, and region, so that changes in practices are further disseminated.

In most other sectors, however, the major decision makers are in fact not academicians. They do not usually read journals reporting research. They have small staffs. In urban areas the most important decision makers may be the mayors of our major cities or cabinet secretaries. In contrast to academic physicians, they do not walk into their offices in the morning, pick up the latest urban studies journal, skim the latest research studies, and talk to their staffs about implementing major findings. This is equally true in the State Department or the Department of the Interior or the Environmental Protection Agency. In these fields, decision makers rely on "experts" to help them. Researchers do not initiate actions.

The implication of this point is that health policy research can be made more useful only if those who conduct it improve their role as experts on current issues—by testifying before Congress, making television and radio appearances, doing background stories for the nation's press, and producing readable syntheses of what research tells us about today's current problems. The most important presentations are those that express the expert's view of the impact of major current trends or public policy changes on the community and what we "know" about the usefulness of past efforts to improve America's health care situation. In the years since the President's Science Advisory Committee report, finding effective health policy solutions has become an immensely more difficult task for government. At the same time it has become its most crucially important task. The work of the authors presented in this volume constitutes a significant step in improving our understanding of how research can be more effectively brought to bear on important policy questions.

The collaboration of these authors under the auspices of the American Enterprise Institute has resulted in a volume that should be of value not only to policy analysts in health but to professional and graduate students in a number of fields—and, most important, to concerned private and public decision makers who must ultimately set the future course of America's medical care.

We should all thank the Pew Foundation for having contributed funds to allow these distinguished authors to combine their talents and insights in developing this volume.

ROBERT J. BLENDON
Senior Vice President
The Robert Wood Johnson Foundation

1. Panel on Health Services Research and Development, President's Science Advisory Committee, Office of Science and Technology, Executive Office of the President, "Improving Health Care through Research and Development" (Washington, D.C., 1972).

Contributors

ROBERT J. BLENDON is a senior vice president at the Robert Wood Johnson Foundation, where he has been for twelve years. He is also on the part-time faculty of Princeton University in the Department of Science and Human Affairs. Previously, he held positions in the Department of Health, Education and Welfare as special assistant to the under secretary and on the staff of the Johns Hopkins Schools of Medicine and Public Health. Dr. Blendon has published extensively in major health journals, including pieces on Medicaid, private giving in health care, medicine in China, and the state of the shortages of physicians and nurses.

LYNN ETHEREDGE is a private consultant in health care financing and policy issues. Most recently he was a senior research associate at the Urban Institute, where his research and writing focused on government health policy issues, the federal budget, and aging. From 1978 to 1982 he directed the Health Branch of the Office of Management and Budget (OMB), where he supervised analyses of national health sector issues and development of recommendations for federal health programs. Mr. Etheredge has held positions in government, at policy research centers, and at universities.

MARION EIN LEWIN is director of AEI's Center for Health Policy Research and of the semiannual Pew Health Policy Program conferences. From 1978 to 1983 she served as associate director of the National Health Policy Forum, a nonpartisan educational program for high-level federal, state, and private-sector specialists in health affairs. She has written on a wide range of subjects in the health care area, including articles and studies on indigent care. She is the editor of *The Health Policy Agenda: Some Critical Questions* (AEI, 1985).

BARBARA BOLLING MANARD joined Lewin and Associates, a Washington-based health policy consulting firm, as a senior consultant in 1981. She has done extensive work in designing a nursing home case-mix reimbursement system for the state of Minnesota and developing financing options for the care of chronically ill children. She has also examined special programs for hospital care of the elderly, the effect of changing Medicaid reimbursement policies on nursing homes, and health manpower. Before joining Lewin and Associates, Dr. Manard held positions as a policy analyst in the Office of the Assistant Secretary for Planning and Evaluation, U.S. Department of Health and Human Services, and as assistant professor of sociology at the University of California, Riverside, and at the University of Virginia.

JOEL MENGES is a Jurgovan & Blair, Inc., associate, with responsibility for performing research, analysis, and documentation tasks on projects of the Management Services Group. His current assignments include HMO Medicare contract proposals, certification applications, and feasibility studies. Before joining JBI in 1985, Mr. Menges was a research associate at the American Enterprise Institute's Center for Health Policy Research, where he participated in evaluations of Medicaid capitation and case management demonstration projects, performed quantitative analyses of government expenditures on social programs, and developed proposals and studies for the health policy center.

IRA MOSCOVICE is associate professor and associate director of the Center for Health Services Research at the University of Minnesota. He has also held positions at the University of Washington and has been a visiting scientist at the Battelle Memorial Institute. He has written extensively on health services research for decision makers, health manpower, rural health care delivery systems, and the effects of federal cutbacks on the health care and insurance loss of disadvantaged groups, including the disabled and families with dependent children.

Introduction

Marion Ein Lewin

In the world of policy making and politics, the discipline of health services research has often experienced rough sledding. Not as widely acclaimed or as well understood as biomedical research, this field, along with many of the other social sciences, has had to struggle for recognition and support. A number of reasons can be cited to explain this state of affairs. In health services research, as opposed to the "hard" sciences, cause and effect are not always readily apparent; the contribution of a specific piece of research to better health care is often difficult to trace.

Health services research has never garnered the powerful constituencies that some other disciplines enjoy. People do not see themselves as immediately affected by the fruits of this kind of research. In health care as in other areas, moreover, support is always easier to rally in behalf of a solution to a particular problem than in the cause of a general area of study.

Perhaps most significant, a chasm of misunderstanding has long existed between researchers and the decision makers who use their product. Policy makers have often perceived researchers as addressing principally other researchers and their aims as obtaining tenure or publishing articles in professional journals. In the eyes of many policy makers, researchers often do not focus on the key questions or write in language that supports decisive action. Researchers feel that decision makers' demands for quick solutions and bottom-line answers, as well as their propensity to mix facts with value judgments, can undermine standards of scientific integrity.

Recent years, however, have witnessed a resurgence of interest in health services research. Efforts have been mounted to make the field more cogent and more relevant by bridging the gap between the spheres of researchers and decision makers. The chapters in this book can be seen as success stories in behalf of these objectives. They not only underscore the key role that health services research can play in shaping new directions in public policy but also show us the potential value of closer collaboration and better communications between social scientists and political actors.

Looking at national health policy over the past fifteen years, Lynn Etheredge, in "Government and Health Care Costs: The Influence of Research on Policy," traces the significant influence of health services research in expanding government and private sector efforts to come to grips with health care financing and delivery and cost containment issues. A number of major federal initiatives during this period—in health professions training, prepaid capitated delivery systems such as health maintenance organizations (HMOs), utilization review, health planning, and technology assessment—stemmed directly from health services research.

According to Etheredge, however, the evolution of health policy research into health policy is not an orderly process. Political realities have often led to the hasty nationwide implementation of new programs based on the research findings available at the time. Later, armed with new information and practical experience, decision makers may ask to reshape or reverse gears on measures once enthusiastically adopted. The lack of orderliness and predictability has other causes. Health research constitutes a vast marketplace of ideas with divergent views about the health care system, about how different reforms would work, and about which outcomes are desirable. The government, contends Etheredge, has nurtured research, but that research has more often than not led to conflicting conclusions about optimal health policy in areas such as the allocation of health resources, HMOs, professional standards review organizations (PSROs), and disease prevention and health promotion.

The author further suggests that the policy debate in health has been in great measure shaped by the competing ideas and frequent rivalry among three disciplines: public health, economics, and medicine. Each has its own ideology and orientation. The public health perspective, that of matching funds with needs, has traditionally been influential in steps taken both to expand and to regulate the supply of health resources. Economics has played a growing role in health policy affairs since the 1970s and has been largely responsible for the dramatic and far-reaching swing to a more competitive, market-oriented health system, based chiefly on incentives rather than regulatory controls. A dominant position in the making of health policy has long been enjoyed by the nation's physicians and medical schools. Only recently has their preeminence begun to be challenged by large purchasers of care wielding increasing power. Over the years the medical profession has been strongly opposed to moves—financial or other—that would interfere with the traditional relationship between physician and patient or would undermine the various missions of academic medical centers.

A theme sounded by Etheredge and echoed by the other authors in the book is that those who labor in the field of health policy analysis and research must always contend with powerful economic, political, and cultural forces. Interest groups exert at least as much influence as the research community on the policy-making process.

One of the most dramatic effects of health policy research has been the development of diagnosis-related groups (DRGs) and their adoption in 1983 as the basis for Medicare's prospective payment system. In "From Health Services Research to Federal Law: The Case of DRGs," Joel Menges points out that this watershed legislation was speedily enacted for a number of reasons. Perhaps most important was the availability of a knowledge base accumulated over many years as the direct result of impressive health services research efforts to develop stronger and more precise hospital payment methods.

Menges reminds us that the inflationary characteristics of Medicare's reasonable-cost formula were already apparent in the early stages of the program. The Social Security Amendments of 1967 sanctioned experiments with alternative methods of reimbursing both institutions and physicians. Sections 222 and 223 of the Social Security Amendments of 1972 marked a further thrust in this direction by authorizing additional testing of prospective and other payment methods. At about this period the government began to finance a group at Yale University that was developing a conceptual framework for identifying a hospital's "output" through the use of a case mix or DRGs. In 1974 New Jersey propelled this concept into practical application by adopting the DRG system as a basis for paying hospitals and thus provided a valuable laboratory for researchers, who were increasingly interested in this payment method as a basis for Medicare hospital fees.

The development and passage into law of the prospective payment system employing DRGs is a fascinating case study of what is possible when policy research and politics are attuned to the same issue. A consensus was growing that relentless double-digit inflation year after year in the hospital industry could no longer be tolerated, that regulatory programs that had been instituted to dampen the cost spiral had been singularly ineffective. The time was ripe to try an entirely new approach to hospital payment. The Reagan administration came to power on a platform of leaner government and market-oriented reforms in health care.

The unusually rapid congressional approval of this fundamental change in Medicare payment was due to other factors as well. Hospitals were operating under the restrictive reimbursement limits mandated by the Tax Equity and Fiscal Responsibility Act (TEFRA) of 1982. Although little was known about the effect DRGs would have on different classes of institutions, an incentive-based prospective payment system seemed on the face of it the lesser of two evils. Minimal time was provided to debate the pros and cons of this far-reaching legislation; less than a month passed between the introduction and passage of the bill that became Public Law 98-21.

If the development of the prospective payment system and DRGs demonstrates the substantial effect health services research can have on the policy-making process, its implementation has provided a fertile field for further research and evaluation. From the very beginning it was clear that DRGs as a hospital payment method would require considerable modification. At the request of Congress, the Prospective Payment Assessment Commission (ProPAC) was created as a nonpartisan, independent group charged with recalibrating DRG rates to reflect changes in treatment patterns, technology, and other factors that may change the relative use of hospital resources. The new payment system has been criticized for not taking sufficiently into account the severity of illness and thereby putting at a disadvantage hospitals that treat sicker patients. The effects of DRGs on access to care and on quality of care remain high-priority concerns and topics of keen interest to researchers. Lively debate continues on how to incorporate payment for capital expenditures into the DRG-based prospective rates. A host of research efforts have been launched to examine the feasibility of developing DRGs for physicians, long-term-care facilities, and mental health services.

The chapters "Health Services Research and the Policy-making Process: State Response to Federal Cutbacks in Programs Affecting Child Health" and "Doing Research for Decision Makers: Nursing Home Reimbursement" present two thought-provoking case studies on brokering health policy research so that it can be used more effectively and persuasively by state decision makers. By coincidence, both focus on efforts spearheaded in Minnesota. Ira Moscovice discusses the role of research in assessing the effects of federal cutbacks on child health and in developing a state response to those reductions. Barbara Manard addresses the pressing issue of the reform of nursing home reimbursement.

A notable trend in recent years has been the states' leadership in charting new health care reforms. As states and localities have been granted greater leeway and responsibility for health care financing and delivery, the need of elected officials and senior program experts for information has escalated. Both are now viewed as active and influential markets for health services research and its products.

4

The Moscovice and Manard articles offer valuable insights into the differences between the culture of research and the realities of the political process. The constraints and opportunities of the policy world place a premium on timely and relevant responses to immediate concerns. The challenge for policy researchers, the authors point out, is to match the scope and design of the research to the subject and to the uses required of the findings. The emphasis, Manard contends, "is more on finding a 'not too badly wrong' answer right now than on finding a 'correct' answer at some later date."

Policy researchers working with decision makers need to recognize that most programs and policies—whether state or federal—are built incrementally and are more likely to be changed by tinkering than by wholesale restructuring. Policy research that argues, however convincingly, for major program overhaul may be of marginal value to elected officials operating within a restricted budget, period of time, and political environment. Moscovice's chapter provides a case in point. He describes Minnesota's interest in expanding maternal and child health services to low-income uninsured families. After considerable analysis and debate, two options were proposed: a statewide insurance pool and Medicaid expansion, both to serve poor pregnant women and children. Medicaid expansion was chosen as the preferred strategy largely because it built on an existing program with an established administrative structure.

High-quality research that is useful to policy makers requires access to good information and reliable data. The rapid pace of change that characterizes today's health care system means that the most relevant and timely information may be found not among published works in university libraries but in a variety of other settings, such as government agencies, trade associations, and consulting firms. As the focus of decision making is increasingly shifted to state and local government, Moscovice stresses, the need arises to develop local data bases and related resources. Unfortunately, data collection and program evaluation have been severely curtailed in recent years because of budget cuts and changing federal policies.

Researchers are called upon throughout this volume to work closely with political actors to learn more about the conditions that stimulate the effective use of research in the making of policy. Among them is the overriding importance of communicating the results of health policy research to decision makers clearly, pertinently, and expeditiously and of maintaining research integrity while simplifying extremely complex information.

The essays in this book indicate that the field of health services research is alive with opportunity. Whereas past policy research was primarily focused on federal programs and policies, today states and

5

local governments, as well as the private sector, are becoming extensive users of this kind of expertise. In an era of limited dollars and growing needs, well-informed decision making has become a premium commodity. Forging a stronger partnership between health policy researchers and decision makers can help us reap the profits.

1
Government and Health Care Costs: The Influence of Research on Policy

Lynn Etheredge

The federal government's growing concern about the costs of health care now dates back almost fifteen years, when it became clear that the acceleration of federal budget and national health costs after the passage of Medicare and Medicaid was not just temporary. The first comprehensive proposals for a health cost strategy were made during the early 1970s. On the advice of health policy experts, the Nixon administration decided that the health care system was in a crisis and presented sweeping proposals for both market and regulatory efforts. The administration envisioned expanding the number of health maintenance organizations (HMOs) from 30 to 1,700 in just five years and enrolling 40 million people by 1976. Its national health insurance plan featured state regulation of hospital budgets and physicians' fees, with federal controls if a state failed to act, and higher cost sharing in private insurance.

In an assessment of what has happened over the past fifteen years, several features stand out.

• The nation did not enact comprehensive health financing reforms, and health care costs have continued to rise rapidly. National health spending, which totaled $75 billion in 1970, passed $400 billion in 1985. The federal government's spending for the Medicare and Medicaid programs grew from $10 billion in 1970 to nearly $95 billion in 1985.

• Without comprehensive federal legislation, progress on structural change of the health care system has been substantial but slow.

After more than a decade of federal development support, HMOs enroll about 7 percent of the population. Four states now have mandatory all-payer hospital rate regulation, and thirty-five states have some form of rate review for at least one class of payer.

• The leading reform ideas still include the encouragement of competition through prepaid systems of care, such as HMOs and preferred provider organizations (PPOs); federal legislation to establish state cost control programs for hospital costs and physicians' fees, with federal controls if the states do not institute them (the Kennedy-Gephardt bill); and increased cost sharing in private insurance.

In retrospect health policy research had conveyed to government officials, even fifteen years ago, the essential points that health care costs were on an uncontrolled, highly inflationary path, that comprehensive, systemic changes were necessary to bring them under control, and that regulation and market incentives should be combined in this effort. Subsequent health research has deepened knowledge of the problem, provided much more solid evidence on the probable results of various reform proposals, and contributed in many ways to policy developments and changes.

We should be dissatisfied, however—and very concerned—about the rate at which the nation's health costs have steadily increased. As professional policy analysts, we all understand that powerful economic, political, and cultural forces enter into the formulation of health policy. Nevertheless, perhaps the most sobering lesson of the past fifteen years is how extraordinarily powerful—and difficult to deal with—those forces are. Looking to the future, we face even greater difficulties in trying to balance the benefits and costs of future growth in the health system.

Health policy research has an important and expanding role in efforts by the government and the private sector to address issues of health financing and costs. This paper offers some information, thoughts, and perspective on the work involved, including the following:

• an overview of how health research has influenced the federal government's policies for dealing with health costs
• a discussion of the chaotic marketplace of ideas about health policy and the changing competitive fortunes of the disciplines involved
• some observations on the processes through which health research is effectively translated into health policy
• a few suggestions about how to draw on lessons of the past so that health research can make even more effective contributions to health policy in the future

Health Policy and Health Policy Research: An Overview

Health policy researchers frequently worry about whether government decision makers will use their work. The lessons of the past fifteen years certainly suggest that this ought not to be a major concern. The federal government has shown an extraordinary interest in research about ways to reduce health care costs and how well such measures work, and a substantial number of reform ideas and research results have found their way into the policy process. Indeed, in retrospect one might wish that federal officials had been somewhat less eager to rush into nationwide implementation of some ideas, such as professional standards review organizations (PSROs), health systems agencies, and diagnosis-related groups (DRGs).

It would be dangerous to conclude, however, that all health policy research has led to the same conclusions about optimal health policy or that it has all been used to advance a common agenda. Indeed, the following review suggests that the influences have often been diverse.[1]

Health Resources: Hospitals, Health Professions, Technology. The nation's hospital bed supply has been a continuing concern of federal health policy, both when it has been seen as inadequate and when it has been seen as excessive. A view that the nation needed more hospital beds led to the enactment of the Hill-Burton program in 1946, and a consensus that the nation had an excess supply led to elimination of the program in 1974. Research on the need to restrain further growth in hospital beds to prevent unnecessary use and higher health costs also gave rise to other measures: the national health planning program in 1974, certificate-of-need legislation in most states (and complementary Section 1122 provisions in the Medicare statute), and national guidelines for hospital supply—four beds per 1,000 population and an 80 percent occupancy rate.[2]

The federal government's programs of aid for training in health professions have also been strongly affected by research findings and the prevailing views on how to restrain health care costs. Starting in the mid-1960s, the federal government sharply increased its financial efforts to overcome shortages and slow the inflation of health care costs by expanding enrollment in schools training students for health professions. Research showing potential savings from the use of professionals who are not physicians led to the addition of such federal programs as aid for physicians' assistants, nurse practitioners, and team dentistry. Evidence that primary care physicians used expensive hospital care less frequently than other specialists gave rise to subsidies for more residency positions for such physicians.

9

As medical school enrollments were starting to peak, research and policy analysis at the Department of Health, Education and Welfare—later formalized in the report of the Graduate Medical Education National Advisory Committee (GMENAC)—concluded that the nation would soon have an oversupply of physicians, particularly in many specialties. These findings were buttressed by other research suggesting that a rising supply of physicians, instead of reducing costs, actually increased national health spending, particularly with fee-for-service billing and the apparent lack of competition in the health care sector. Consequently, by the early 1980s cost considerations led to the elimination of most federal assistance programs for training in health professions and to limitation of the entry of foreign medical graduates.[3]

Medical technology has long been recognized as having a major role both in improving health care and in increasing costs. Concerns about the need for more research on the cost effectiveness of new medical technology led to the establishment of the National Center for Health Care Technology. Under a different administration, however, concern that such research could slow technological innovation and cost reductions helped terminate the center. The roles of the Office of Technology Assessment and the National Academy of Sciences in technology assessment have recently been expanded.[4]

Health Planning. Health policy research has also played a role both in the initial development of health planning activities and in the subsequent disenchantment with them. Inadequacies of the Comprehensive Health Planning voluntary program led to far more regulatory planning legislation in 1974, with a nationwide system of certificate-of-need requirements, health systems agencies, state health planning and development agencies, and state health coordinating councils. Several years later, however, studies evaluating these new efforts found that health planning was usually ineffective in controlling capital expenditures. Similarly, advocates of greater competition in the health sector argued that, where health planning was effective, it actually raised costs by protecting the franchises of unneeded and inefficient hospitals. Federal support for health planning has been sharply curtailed.[5]

Health Maintenance Organizations. The federal government's nationwide effort to expand HMOs in the 1970s was based on research showing that they produced substantial savings for their patients. After more than a decade of further research, the savings claims still seem valid. Nevertheless, research has also highlighted "adverse selection"—the tendency of people to enroll in HMOs only when they will gain financially. Such selection makes it difficult for the Medicare program and employers to save money when they offer HMO coverage as an option. Moreover, although the expansion of HMO enrollment was impressive, it fell far short of the optimistic expectations that HMOs would become the model for mainstream medical care. In conformity with the Catch-22 of program evaluation—that programs are either judged successful and recommended for termination for having fulfilled their purpose or judged unsuccessful and recommended for termination for not having fulfilled their purpose— the HMO development program was phased out for having successfully demonstrated a cost-saving option.[6]

Professional Standards Review Organizations. Research has played a role both in new utilization review initiatives and in subsequent disillusionment with those initiatives. In the early 1970s, data on the Medicare program showed substantial regional differences in admissions and lengths of stay. Limited data from pilot projects suggested that major savings could be obtained by removing utilization review from hospitals and fiscal intermediaries and turning it over to external organizations of physicians. Subsequently, formal evaluations conducted by the Department of Health and Human Services (HHS) and the Congressional Budget Office showed that PSROs were not cost effective and led to proposals to abolish them and to their reorganization into professional review organizations (PROs).[7]

Prevention. Research on the possibilities of preventing poor health, partly stimulated by Canada's Lalonde report, led the Department of Health and Human Services, particularly its Centers for Disease Control, to do extensive work in the late 1970s to arrive at nationally achievable goals in a number of areas. But health services research has also raised doubts about available techniques for changing individual behavior and has thus moderated enthusiasm for government-sponsored efforts to implement those goals.[8]

Health Care Financing. Much of the research into health care costs has focused on the financing of health care, and as a result most of its important aspects are better understood. There is little disagreement today with the propositions that health service providers respond to financial incentives, that open-ended payment of hospitals and physicians is inflationary, or that payment by third parties helps to increase health care costs.

Studies of state hospital rate-setting commissions have produced a fairly broad body of evidence that they can be workable and save money and analyses of a number of the technical issues in their

11

design. Such research contributed directly to the adoption of a prospective hospital payment system for the Medicare program in the Tax Equity and Fiscal Responsibility Act of 1982.[9]

One of the most dramatic outcomes of health policy research has been the development of DRGs and their adoption as the basis for Medicare hospital fees in the 1983 social security legislation. Now that the system is being implemented, a great deal of research is under way to evaluate its effectiveness and to assist in the midcourse corrections necessary to deal with technological change, severity adjustments, productivity targets, unbundling, volume adjustments, capital and teaching costs, and the combination of hospital, regional, and national weights.[10]

No review of how health research has influenced policy should fail to mention the Rand health insurance experiment. Costing nearly $100 million and more than ten years of effort, it was the major research project of the 1970s. The study established, with an authority that is unlikely to be seriously questioned, that out-of-pocket costs significantly affect the use of health care services. The study seems destined to have a major impact on both government programs and private health insurance.[11]

Research on long-term care has also led to important cost containment initiatives and to policy reversals. Through the early 1970s a strong element of policy thought held that adding coverage of less expensive services would reduce overall health costs—that coverage of outpatient care, for example, would be more than offset by lower hospital expenses. Research on the number of people inappropriately hospitalized who could be served in less expensive settings brought about the expansion of nursing home benefits. The number of people inappropriately placed in skilled nursing facilities who could be served in less expensive settings led to the expansion of benefits for intermediate-care facilities. And the number of people in all three types of institutions who could be served outside institutions led to rapid growth of home health and related home services. But subsequent research on such developments also suggested that lower per unit costs do not save money if volume increases, as it often did. Today conventional wisdom would probably be summarized as "an add-on service is an add-on cost," and policy makers are extremely reluctant to expand long-term-care benefits in any major way.[12]

In contrast to the development of research and policy in other areas, the physicians' market and alternative fee-for-service payment policies have received much less attention. This phenomenon still puzzles me. One explanation is that all the administrations in the 1970s believed that existing evidence already showed that current policies—based on "usual, customary, and reasonable" reimbursement—were clearly wrong and should be replaced with regulated fee schedules. Other factors have been the exceptional difficulty of obtaining adequate data for such research and the inadequate explanatory models for physicians' behavior and pricing decisions.[13]

Despite all the action, controversy, and chaos, the past fifteen years have produced a much more reliable research base for government policy. Except for payment of physicians, nearly every major idea on the political spectrum about how to restrain health costs has been tested. Research has played a key role in bringing these ideas forth as credible proposals and has frequently provided reliable evidence about how much more limited the results often prove in reality than the original proponents claimed or hoped. As a result we now have a more reliable book on major issues in the control of health costs, particularly the three major strategies of state hospital rate setting, HMOs, and cost sharing.

The Intellectual Ferment

The evolution of health policy research and health policy described in the previous section has been far from predictable or even orderly.[14] Views about the health care system, the possible effects of reforms, and the desirable courses of action have diverged widely, even wildly.

There is no simple way to make sense of this chaos or of the apparent lack of resolution of many issues unless we see the marketplace of policy ideas as probably the most intensely competitive and rapidly changing feature of the health care system. It includes not only many different customers (with different preferences) but also many suppliers and products. And while these interelite disputes have raged, the evolution of the health system has usually proceeded quite independently of the intellectual policy debate about what should be happening. Nevertheless, for present purposes we can usefully sort out what has been going on as being shaped by three academic-professional disciplines, two ideologies, and a recurrent idea reemerging in different forms.

The Academic and Professional Wars. Many health policy debates can usefully be read as involving competition among three major academic-professional traditions: public health, economics, and medicine.

The public health tradition has been largely concerned with determining the needs of groups of people and matching resources to those needs. It has thus been most influential in efforts both to expand and to regulate the supply of health resources and to change the organization of health care. The health planning program and its

13

guidelines, as well as the analyses of the supply of health professionals by GMENAC and others, could be described as having their intellectual home in this tradition. Proposals for government-sponsored reorganization of the health system, such as more primary care, community health centers, and prepaid group practice, can also be associated with this way of thinking about health policy. Such contributions were a rich source of government health policy and programs well into the 1970s.

The influence of economics on health policy began growing early in the 1970s. Economists, usually by nature as well as by professional indoctrination, are suspicious of professionally determined needs and their use in prescribing the available supply and organization of services. They tend to emphasize notions of consumer sovereignty, investigate how actors are and can be influenced by economic motives, and suggest widespread use of financial incentives rather than regulation.

Such ideas have been controversial in the health policy arena, particularly among public health professions. Notions of encouraging physicians and hospitals to respond to anything other than their professional judgments or the sharing of costs by patients as a "barrier" between patients and providers have occasionally been viewed as reprehensible. Policy proposals whose intellectual home is in this economic tradition have included cost sharing by patients, DRGs and other prospective payment systems with incentives, vouchers, and competition through HMOs and PPOs. Also in this tradition are critiques of health planning and of market-distorting demand and supply subsidies, ranging from tax treatment of employers' health insurance contributions to government programs for increasing the supply of health professionals.

Some observers may view the growing role of economic concepts in shaping government health policy as evidence that economics is inherently superior to other disciplines in addressing health policy issues. A different view would be that the public health tradition is most useful for problems of unmet needs and resource shortages and economics more useful for problems of excess supply and the consequent economic behavior of an industry undergoing rapid financial and organizational changes and increasingly competing to attract business. As the size and nature of the health sector have changed, so too have the ideas on government policies to deal with it.

Medicine is the third major profession whose ways of thinking about health care strongly influence health policy. The view of medical schools and physicians of optimal national health policy could be summarized as (1) find the best people to be physicians and give them the best training; (2) get physicians and patients together; and (3) have everyone else do (and pay for) what the physician decides is best for the patient.

Although public health and economics professionals have built a strong case about the problems of this view and debated (frequently against one another) about how to restructure the health system, the evolution and enormous growth of the health sector have largely come about as a result of how physicians view medical care. Perhaps one measure of the ascendancy of the medical profession is that it has not yet even had to field an intellectual champion to justify its role. Indeed, government health policy in the 1970s and 1980s, through PSROs and PROs, has strengthened the physicians' power to determine appropriate medical care.

Opposing Ideologies. The policy debates produced by professional rivalries have been further complicated by passionate political ideologies. Perhaps because health care is so important and still at issue, it has been a particular focus for those who believe that the government's role must be sharply expanded or cut back. Proposals as divergent as nationalizing the health care system and cashing out existing government programs through vouchers were both strongly advocated in the 1970s, and supporting research results were assembled by all the parties. In such an atmosphere research was frequently used to advance or attack ideological agendas. Viable and enactable proposals for addressing health costs were frequently of secondary importance to committed participants, and reasonable compromises were often difficult or impossible to achieve.

A Recurrent Idea. Most reform ideas of the past fifteen years have been built around the need to manage hospitals' and physicians' services within limited budgets. Many policy debates during this period should be read less as discussions of fundamentally new ideas than as disputes about assigning the management role to one or another actor in the health care system. The HMO creates a new organization to undertake this management role; the independent practice association uses medical societies; vouchers let the individual manage his own care; capitation payments allocate the management responsibility to a "gatekeeper" physician. Advocates of community health centers (CHCs) envision an optimal health system with CHC managers. Others see the community hospital managing the budgets and resources for areawide health care or tertiary care centers as headquarters for a regionalized health system. Organizational arrangements now being debated include having the employer take the

15

lead in negotiating and arranging for health services (through PPOs) and assigning such a role to health insurance companies, as recently proposed by the Midwest Business Group on Health. Some national health insurance proposals advocate the federal government as the best overall manager, while state rate-setting proposals assign that role to state governments and community maxicaps to local communities. Over the past fifteen years, nearly every actor in the health system has had an advocate for reorganizing the health system to provide it with management authority over hospitals' and physicians' services.

Since most of these models can and do coexist, it is unclear whether public policy ever will—or should—choose to exclude any of them. Nevertheless, we should be able to draw a useful lesson from these debates. Reform proposals are often less about real health care issues and more about the autonomy, status, and income of existing actors (particularly in relation to one another) than one would surmise from reading the intellectual arguments about the issues supposedly being discussed.

How Health Research Becomes Health Policy

The past fifteen years have seen the development of a very effective, though informal, communication network for bringing health policy research, ideas, and proposals into the government decision-making processes. For those interested in health policy research, how and how well those processes work are a matter of continuing interest.

Few presidents, HHS secretaries, senators and congressmen, or corporate executives spend much time reading academic journals. They depend mostly on their staffs and on selected advisers, particularly (for legislators) among their constituents. Since few can be trusted advisers to decision makers, the importance of having strong, experienced professional staffs who can mediate between researchers and decision makers cannot be overemphasized. Such staffs learn the issues, options, and facts, monitor developments, request specific policy research, and distill the information for the decision makers for whom they work. Successful translation of research into policy requires communicating with the people in these staff positions and paying attention to their concerns.

Three kinds of institutions facilitate this process for the federal government: the National Health Policy Forum, specialized publications, and health policy consulting and research centers. Washington-based lobbying activities by the health sector have also grown explosively.

The National Health Policy Forum has played a key role for more than a decade in bringing researchers and health sector professionals to Washington for meetings with congressional and executive branch staff. The forum has been a major factor in ensuring a timely, balanced flow of information into the policy process, both through these meetings and in the flyers it circulates, which provide background information on health policy issues.

A second communication medium that has developed rapidly in recent years consists of specialized publications, often based in the Washington area. These newsletters and journals collect and disseminate information of particular interest to health policy staff.

Finally, policy research centers and policy consulting firms have an increasingly important role in the transmission of knowledge. HHS, for example, has made long-term arrangements with several research centers for continuing assistance in health policy analyses. A number of policy research firms, many of whom employ former government researchers and analysts, also assist government decision makers. These firms also transmit expertise on health cost issues developed in Washington over the past decade to state governments and corporate actors who are becoming involved in health policy.

Despite the record of the past fifteen years and the government's increasing need to address rising health care costs, the communication between research and policy may not flow as smoothly in the future. As those familiar with the problem know, recent reductions in staff have lowered the capacity of several government offices to address issues of health costs. The workload of remaining staff members is particularly heavy, and the burden on several perennially understaffed committees and offices has increased as the government legislates new, complex Medicare and Medicaid legislation and is besieged by policy analyses from lobbyists. The capacity of government staffs to escape from such day-to-day pressures is increasingly strained. All involved will need to work at the communication process.

Conclusion

Nearly twenty years after the enactment of Medicare and Medicaid, the federal government has recently broken the link between Medicare's payments to hospitals and physicians and what these providers ask to be paid. The government and the $400 billion health industry are thus on the threshold of what will be an increasingly and intensely conflictual process for dealing with health care costs. Health policy research may be able to make very important contributions to the multibillion-dollar decisions that lie ahead. A few suggestions follow.

17

• First, researchers must continue to emphasize that the nation's health cost problems have systemic roots and require systemic change. We have a responsibility to provide consumer warning labels for the latest brands of snake oil so that decision makers are dissuaded from believing that the answers are easy and quick or that a new program wrinkle or a few more years for markets to develop will solve the problem.

• Second, researchers can contribute by continuing to bring forth evidence on how the health system is treating uninsured and vulnerable populations and institutions. These groups cannot afford high-priced lobbyists, and research is needed to make sure that reliable information on their problems is available in the decision process.

• Third, better data systems must be devised to serve both policy researchers and payers for health service. As many government officials and business groups have discovered, they have almost no ability to monitor and assess many cost and quality developments because relevant, timely data are not available. Researchers should play a major role in the design of national, statewide, and areawide data systems that can be used to improve research, cost and quality, regulation, and competition. Such data will be needed particularly by the federal government as it begins to monitor much more complex developments in health care, such as the responses to DRGs and systems for setting physicians' fees.

• Fourth, a major challenge is to develop more reliable guides on the contributions that various competitive and regulatory measures can make to balancing costs and benefits for different types of services in different market environments and to evaluating major changes in payment policies and in providers' behavior.

• Finally, researchers must communicate their findings and insights effectively to a rapidly expanding audience of those in the private sector and in state and local governments who make decisions about health financing issues, as well as to federal officials and their staffs.

Notes

1. The wealth of health policy research and writing over the fifteen years makes it impossible to acknowledge all the major contributions in this brief essay. References cited below are representative of the literature.

2. A general review of American health policy through 1980, which covers national hospital construction policy, is Paul Starr, *The Social Transformation of American Medicine* (New York: Basic Books, 1982).

3. U.S. Department of Health and Human Services, *Graduate Medical Education National Advisory Commission Report*, 1980.

4. David Blumenthal, "Federal Policy toward Health Care Technology: The Case of the National Center," *Milbank Memorial Fund Quarterly*, vol. 4 (1983), pp. 584–613.

5. Thomas Bice, "Health Planning and Regulation Effects on Hospital Costs," *Annual Review of Public Health* (1980), no. 1, pp. 137–61.

6. Harold Luft, *Health Maintenance Organizations: Dimensions of Performance* (New York: Wiley Interscience, 1981).

7. Allen Dobson et al., "PSROs: Their Current Status and Their Impact to Date," *Inquiry*, vol. 15, no. 2 (June 1978), pp. 113–28.

8. U.S. Department of Health and Human Services, *Healthy People: The Surgeon General's Report on Health Promotion and Disease Prevention*, 1979.

9. Brian Biles, Carl Schramm, and J. Graham Atkinson, "Health Cost Inflation under State Rate-setting Programs," *New England Journal of Medicine*, vol. 303 (1980), p. 664.

10. Prospective Payment Assessment Commission, *Report and Recommendations to the Secretary, U.S. Department of Health and Human Services, April 1, 1985*, and *Technical Appendices*, 1985.

11. Joseph Newhouse et al., "Some Interim Results from a Controlled Trial of Cost Sharing," *New England Journal of Medicine*, vol. 305 (1981), p. 1501.

12. Bruce Vladeck, *Unloving Care: The Nursing Home Tragedy* (New York: Basic Books, 1980).

13. Lynn Etheredge, *Medicare: Paying the Physician—History, Issues, Options*, U.S. Senate Special Committee on Aging, S. Rpt. 98–153, 1984.

14. I am indebted to Lloyd Etheredge for encouraging me to think about the role of research in government learning. See Lloyd Etheredge, "Government Learning: An Overview," in Samuel Long, ed., *Handbook of Political Behavior* (New York: Plenum, 1981), vol. 2, pp. 73–161.

2

From Health Services Research to Federal Law: The Case of DRGs

Joel Menges

The enactment of Medicare's prospective payment system (PPS) in March 1983 marked a revolutionary change in federal reimbursement policy for inpatient hospital care. PPS introduced a per case pricing system, with payments to hospitals based on 467 diagnosis-related groups (DRGs). Payments are no longer based on a hospital's costs of treating all its patients. Instead, each DRG payment amount is intended to reflect the average cost of treating a specific illness in all hospitals. If a hospital is successful in keeping its costs below the average, it will profit from the new payment system; if not, it will suffer financially. Thus PPS provides a sharp contrast to the retrospective, cost-based reimbursement system that had been in effect since Medicare's inception in 1965.

Despite the major departure of PPS from past policy and its rapid enactment by Congress, the new system has several evolutionary aspects. It can be viewed as the most recent step in a process that began in 1972; since then the federal government has become increasingly concerned over the spiraling cost of the health care it purchases for its elderly citizens. Specifically, inpatient hospital expenditures, which accounted for about two-thirds of Medicare outlays

This paper is largely the product of interviews with three persons instrumental in the formation of Medicare's prospective payment system: Gerard Anderson, formerly of the Office of the Secretary at the U.S. Department of Health and Human Services (HHS) and now associate director of the Center for Hospital Finance and Management at Johns Hopkins University; Allen Dobson, acting director of the Office of Research and Demonstrations at the Health Care Financing Administration; and Clifton Gaus, former director of Medicare research at HHS and current president of the Foundation for Health Services Research. I also thank Marion Ein Lewin of the American Enterprise Institute and Glenn Hackbarth of Intermountain Health Care for carefully reviewing the paper. The paper was initially a joint project with Marie Hackbarth who, despite a career change, put in much of the background work and helped shape the revisions. I take full responsibility for any inaccuracies or misrepresentations.

and rose at an average annual rate of 17 percent between 1968 and 1982, became the focus of the government's efforts to gain some control over its Medicare outlays. This paper reviews the development of hospital cost regulation, focusing on the relationship between policy makers and researchers in shaping the development of PPS.

The Historical Development of the Prospective Payment System

The 1972 Social Security Amendments. The 1972 social security amendments laid the groundwork for prospective payment of hospital care. Section 222 of the amendments authorized the federal government to finance and evaluate demonstrations by the states of alternative ways of reimbursing hospitals. This marked the birth of state rate-setting programs except in New York, which had developed a rate-setting program on its own in 1970. Efforts to contain hospital costs during the mid-1970s were undertaken primarily by the states. The states' programs usually included careful review of hospital budgets and regulations limiting the rate of increase in each hospital's inpatient costs.

Section 223 of the social security amendments stipulated that Medicare would not pay an "unreasonable amount" for health care. The Social Security Administration (SSA), which was the administrative agency for Medicare at the time—the Health Care Financing Administration (HCFA) took over administration of the program in 1977—interpreted this to mean that the government could set an upper limit on the amount it would pay for health care services under Medicare.

The initial Medicare reimbursement regulations stemming from the Section 223 amendments, put in place in 1974, set per diem limits on routine hospital costs such as bed, board, and nursing care. Ancillary costs, however, were not included in the per diem limits. The per diem limit on routine costs for each hospital was based on classifications of bed size, urban or rural location, and per capita income in the hospital's area. There were four bed size classifications for urban hospitals, three for rural. Hospitals with more beds had a higher per diem limit than those with fewer beds, urban limits were higher than rural, and areas with high per capita incomes had higher limits. The dollar amount of the adjustments was determined by the SSA and later by the HCFA, although the rationale for adjusting for these factors stemmed from the body of research on hospital cost functions.

Regardless of which classification a hospital fell into, the initial limits were set fairly high, and very few hospitals were affected. The government realized that such a liberal limit would do little to contain costs and conversely might create incentives for hospitals to increase their costs until they reached the limit. Therefore, over the next few years it gradually tightened the per diem limits. Through this process the regulations became somewhat more effective; the government no longer reimbursed every hospital for every dollar billed.[1]

On the whole, however, the per diem system was conspicuously ineffective. The growth in Medicare inpatient hospital expenditures continued to accelerate through the mid-1970s, averaging over 20 percent per year. Two particular concerns were the absence of restrictions on the use of ancillaries and the reimbursement of unnecessarily long lengths of stay at the same rate as appropriate stays. Thus a profligate hospital using an excessive amount of ancillary services or keeping patients hospitalized longer than was medically necessary would receive considerably more Medicare revenue per patient than its more efficient counterpart.

Although it was commonly known that the per diem limits rewarded inefficient behavior, little was known about how to identify the inefficient institutions. Some hospitals might argue, for example, that their high costs were due not to inefficiency but to a more severe case mix and to expenses related to teaching.

The research conducted at that time to measure efficiency in hospitals had not given policy makers a clear answer. Most of it had by necessity classified hospitals into "like" groups and then measured the costs of each hospital in relation to those of its peers. There was little consensus, however, about which factors should differentiate the peer groups or how each factor should be weighted. Each study used some combination of what were thought to be the major determinants of cost differences among hospitals: bed size; rural-urban classification; public, private nonprofit, or private for-profit status; wage indexes; teaching costs; percentage of charity care and bad debt; and classification by case mix or severity of illness.

A few hospitals were consistently found to be either efficient or inefficient providers, regardless of the factors and formulas used. But most hospitals were not so easily categorized. Their status fluctuated widely with the criteria that were applied. Nonetheless, this research led to a consensus that reimbursement of hospitals must be adjusted in some way for case mix.

Measuring Case Mix. The first federal action reflecting an interest in case mix as a factor in reimbursement occurred in 1974, when the Social Security Administration provided continued funding to the research taking place at Yale University. The Yale group, under an earlier grant from the National Center for Health Services Research, had been developing a conceptual framework—using DRGs—for identifying a hospital's "output." Up to this point, their method was intended not to become the basis for any sort of reimbursement scheme but simply to help hospitals improve internal management.

Interest in case mix reimbursement was boosted when New Jersey surprised the federal government in 1976 with a proposal to use the Yale DRG method as the primary factor in determining hospital reimbursement. The Carter administration, however, continued to pursue methods based on state rate-setting programs (such as Maryland's). These programs may have included a case mix adjustment, but reimbursement levels were primarily determined through rigorous budget review.

Although per case payments were not on the policy agenda of the Carter administration, it had a keen interest in adjusting the Section 223 limits equitably for case mix. Thus research on hospitals' case mix continued, identifying wide variations in both the kinds of patients treated in different hospitals and the rates different hospitals were charging for the same diagnosis. These findings supported the argument for reimbursing on the basis of case mix.

Increased Budget Pressure. When the fiscally conservative Reagan administration took office in 1981, political pressure increased to change a cost-based system that was rewarding inefficiency and contributing to the spiraling costs of health care. In 1982, with Medicare inpatient hospital expenditures having risen by 19 percent per year for the past three years, the administration began to develop prospective payment options. After the Tax Equity and Fiscal Responsibility Act (TEFRA) of 1982 was passed, the question was no longer whether prospective payment would be enacted but when and in what form.

The Tax Equity and Fiscal Responsibility Act of 1982. Although the Medicare changes under TEFRA perpetuated the cost-based system and many of its defects, the bill marked an important step in the evolution of hospital cost regulation. Its provisions eliminated many of the disincentives for efficient behavior, introduced a case mix adjustment, and required the Department of Health and Human Services (HHS) to provide Congress with a legislative proposal for prospective payment for inpatient hospital services.

TEFRA replaced the per diem limit on routine costs with a per discharge limit that was extended to cover ancillary as well as routine services. Although TEFRA removed incentives to increase the length of stay or to use ancillary services excessively, it preserved incentives

23

for hospitals to increase their costs until their discharge limits were reached. Hospitals that collected Medicare revenue in excess of their per discharge limits had to return the difference to the government, while hospitals whose Medicare charges fell below their limits were given a small incentive payment. The incentive payments marked the first reward for efficient behavior in the history of Medicare reimbursement,[2] but hospitals were better off if they increased their costs to the limits than if they stayed below them and obtained the incentive payment.

The new limits for each hospital were based on its costs in a base year. For the first time, however, a case mix factor was included in the calculation of a hospital's limit. This change was designed to ensure that hospitals treating more seriously ill patients would receive higher reimbursements. Each hospital was assigned a Medicare case mix index determined by the severity of the cases it treated. The per discharge limits were then adjusted by this index to arrive at an overall limit for each hospital. The DRG method developed at Yale and employed in the New Jersey demonstration was used to make the adjustment.

Under TEFRA the rate by which a hospital's limit could increase was also constrained. The rate of increase was calculated by using another tool of federal reimbursement policy—the hospital market basket. This index, measuring annual increases in hospital input prices, is used annually to adjust the TEFRA limits. It was later used for the original calculation and subsequent updating of the DRG rates.[3]

Taken as a whole, the new limits under TEFRA were much more stringent than the previous restrictions. More services fell under them; they were tightened so that more hospitals would be affected; and the rate at which they could increase was also constrained.

One issue raised by the TEFRA limits was that the wrong hospitals might be squeezed. This had been a problem for the government since the passage of the Section 223 social security amendments. The system of limits could easily be used to reduce government expenditures by setting the limits at a level where the desired budget savings would be achieved. But the resulting concerns were that the quality of care might sometimes be affected or that hospitals whose higher costs were often legitimate given their teaching burden or severe case mix, for example, would be unfairly penalized.

In the past the government had responded to these concerns by adjusting the limits to account for such factors equitably. Neither the providers nor the government, however, seemed satisfied that the underlying issues were being effectively addressed. Traditionally, any hospital affected by the limits argued that it was being underreimbursed for legitimate high costs. The government suspected that many hospitals at or near the limits were manipulating the regulations to maximize their reimbursement. From 1972 to 1982 the government had engaged in what it perceived as a losing battle with providers, and the Reagan administration saw no hope of reversing the situation through continued use of limits.

Prospective payment systems had tremendous appeal. They enabled the government to pay a flat, predetermined amount per admission, per case, per procedure, or per beneficiary—then let the efficient providers keep the difference and force inefficient ones to absorb the loss. Any prospective payment system would still require adjustments for teaching, capital, and whatever other factors were determined to create legitimate variances in hospital costs. Nevertheless, the administration was confident that this approach was preferable to perpetuating the inefficiencies and inequities of the cost-based system.

The Development of the HHS Proposal. The development of PPS in 1982 had two components—the selection of the DRG method over other options and the details concerning implementation of the system. The larger decision—selecting the case mix method—was made by Richard Schweiker, then HHS secretary. Other alternatives considered included a per capita payment, or voucher, and a per discharge payment.

Although the capitation, or voucher, alternative enjoyed considerable popularity in the administration and was often viewed as a potential end point in experimentation with Medicare reimbursement, it was rejected because it could not be put into place quickly, if at all, in most parts of the country. It required the willingness and ability of insurers and providers to accept the full risk of incurring costs greater than the per capita amount. A voluntary voucher, which would have allowed Medicare enrollees to choose between Medicare and alternative health plans, was also considered but was rejected because of fears that proportionally more healthy beneficiaries would select the voucher. The government's outlays would then have increased because it would have had not only to continue to pay for the health services for its unhealthy beneficiaries but also to purchase insurance plans for its healthy beneficiaries. The HCFA is closely evaluating health maintenance organizations (HMOs) that have enrolled a large number of Medicare beneficiaries under a per capita rate. HMO enrollment selection under the recently enacted Medicare risk-contracting program will serve as an indication of the feasibility of the capitation system.

Under the per discharge option, a hospital would have received a single, predetermined payment applied to all discharges. This option could have been implemented nationally and was attractive because of its simplicity. Nevertheless, it was rejected because of concerns about case mix. Although the flat rate could have been adjusted for case mix, paying the same amount for seriously and marginally ill patients had dangerous implications for access to care for beneficiaries with severe health problems.

Conversely, the DRG method did account for case mix and had been refined to the point where it was deemed ready for national implementation. In addition, the New Jersey demonstration, which applied DRG payment to all payers, was faring well. Although the New Jersey experiment had some important differences from the national HHS proposal, its initial success strengthened the argument for reimbursing according to DRGs.

Once the DRG pricing system was selected, the remaining details of the HHS proposal were worked out fairly rapidly. Decisions to pass through direct teaching and capital costs (that is, to continue adjusting for them) facilitated the fine-tuning process. During this period the HCFA's Office of Research and Demonstrations helped shape the details of PPS through extensive simulation research designed to measure the distributional effects of the proposal on various kinds of hospitals. This research led, for example, to doubling the indirect teaching adjustment and to including an outlier provision, which reimbursed for some patients outside the DRG system. The outlier provision protected smaller hospitals against the adverse financial effects of having one or more cases that were much more costly than the average patient in a DRG category; it thereby preserved hospitals' incentives to admit and provide adequate treatment to severely ill patients.

A final noteworthy provision is that PPS required hospitals to accept the DRG rates as payment in full. This provision protected beneficiaries from the additional charges to which they were exposed before the adoption of PPS.

Swift Congressional Action. The administration delivered its proposal to Congress in December 1982. Congress then moved with uncharacteristic, if not unheard of, speed by enacting PPS in March 1983. The quick passage of PPS was attributable to four factors: (1) widespread acknowledgment of the inadequacy of the system it was replacing; (2) the ability of HHS to implement the program rapidly; (3) the perception by hospitals that TEFRA's limits were draconian and that PPS would be the lesser of two evils; and (4) perhaps most important, the attachment of PPS to a popular bipartisan bill to rescue social security.

26

Congress made some noteworthy changes in the administration's proposal, although they were chiefly worked out through significant consultation with the same HHS officials who had shaped the original proposal. In most respects Congress watered down the HHS proposal, by, for example, phasing it in over four years, increasing the percentage of outliers from 1 percent to 5–6 percent, and adding a second regional adjustment factor. The administration had proposed a stringent system in the belief that if it had recommended a phase-in or a greater number of outliers, Congress would simply have used that as the base from which to begin compromising.

Health Services Research and the Development of PPS

The retrospective, cost-based reimbursement system, despite its well-documented shortcomings, remained in place for more than a decade. This suggests a somewhat unsuccessful link between research findings and policy outcomes. Yet the policy makers had little choice except to preserve the status quo—however inadequate—until the research on a workable alternative was completed.

In the meantime the government focused on adjusting the Section 223 limits to reflect more equitably hospital cost differences caused by such factors as location, case mix, and teaching. Research findings also contributed heavily to this process. Teaching adjustments, wage indexes, and similar efforts to account for the diversity among hospitals were not made until research exposed the inequities of not adjusting for these factors.

Given the overwhelming complexities involved in paying hospitals, policy makers have become increasingly eager to finance research on hospitals' costs and behavior. A recent indication of the policy makers' growing reliance on research was the long shopping list of congressionally mandated studies included in the bill enacting PPS. The final section of this paper describes the continuing role of research in PPS.

Whatever importance one attaches to the research that went into the enactment of PPS, researchers will play a prominent role in the future of the program. Research findings will be heavily relied on in three interrelated areas: program refinement, program expansion, and program evaluation.

Refinement Issues. According to the law, the PPS rates must be updated annually, and the weights among DRGs must be recalculated as deemed necessary. The first recalibration is scheduled for fiscal year 1986. In addition, DRGs have highlighted the importance of more accurately determining the effects on hospitals of teaching costs,

27

capital expenditures, and free care. In attempting to determine adequate and equitable payment for these factors, the government must also decide whether these costs should be passed through (reimbursed separately from the DRG rates) or whether they can and should be built into the rates.

Recognizing the importance of sound, objective analysis in making these revisions, Congress created the Prospective Payment Assessment Commission (ProPAC), a nonpartisan, independent group responsible for evaluating the DRG rates and weights. An often expressed fear is that, despite the initial requirement of budget neutrality (through fiscal year 1985), the DRG rates will eventually be used as a means to create budget savings, with hospitals squeezed to the point where they cannot maintain quality of care. The extent to which ProPAC's recommendations about the rate and weight recalibrations are followed could be the crucial test of the administration's and Congress's willingness to manipulate the system to generate budget savings.

There are concerns about both the accuracy and the timeliness of the data available to ProPAC for revising the rates and recalibrating the weights. Although the DRG weights are intended to reflect differences in a hospital's *costs* of treating different cases, the government's data are on hospital *charges*. Because of the high degree of cross-subsidization (among both procedures and payment sources) practiced in hospitals, charges and costs are generally regarded as poorly correlated. To the extent that they are, the DRG weights will fail to adjust equitably for the different costs a hospital experiences in treating different cases.

The timeliness of the recalibrations continues to be a source of criticism. Fiscal year 1981 data were used to calculate the fiscal year 1984 DRG rates (using the hospital market basket to adjust for inflation), and fiscal year 1981 data determine the weighting of DRGs until fiscal year 1986. Critics argue that using a two- to three-year-old snapshot of the rapidly changing system as the basis for current policy will always make reimbursement off the mark.

The administration, though acknowledging these shortcomings in the data, responds that the situation will improve not by waiting but by implementing a PPS system that forces hospitals to pay close attention to their actual costs per case. PPS will clearly generate better data in hospitals, but the extent to which those data will be shared with the government is not known.

In defending its new payment system, the administration also points to research indicating that DRGs adjust adequately for hospitals' varying costs. Two analysts at the HCFA who addressed this issue concluded that the DRG case mix method "provides a valid and generally accurate representation of the expected costliness of an individual hospital's patient mix."[4] If this research had exposed a poor correlation between the DRG case mix and hospital costs, the HHS would probably not have chosen to push PPS. Nevertheless, questions concerning the extent to which the DRG weights reflect a hospital's costs for its case mix merit close attention by researchers.

The adjustments and allowances for teaching costs, capital costs, and wage indexes took on heightened importance under budget neutrality, where one hospital's gain must come at the expense of another. For example, when it was learned (through simulation research at the HCFA and the Congressional Budget Office) that a majority of the teaching hospitals would lose revenue under PPS, the adjustment for indirect teaching costs was doubled.[5] This change made PPS appear more equitable in the eyes of the teaching hospitals. But it was financed at the expense of the smaller, nonteaching institutions, many of which were rural hospitals already scheduled to receive lower payments because of the difference between urban and rural wages. Rural hospitals located just outside a standard metropolitan statistical area (SMSA) contend that they are especially shortchanged by the adjustments to the DRG rates since they have the same high wage costs as hospitals in the neighboring SMSA but receive lower rates.

Policy makers are still wrestling with developing mechanisms for Medicare's treatment of capital expenditures. Debate continues over whether to include or exclude return on equity for proprietary hospitals and interest on funded depreciation for voluntary hospitals. Other issues include the phasing-in of capital cost additions and whether those should be for specific hospitals or based on national trends. Moreover, ways in which hospitals should be reimbursed for rendering care to a disproportionate share of low-income persons have yet to be determined. The fiscal year 1986 budget will include those adjustments.

Because the adjustment process identifies winners and losers, it poses political as well as technical problems. The losers will lobby for higher adjustments, which may well be dictated by political influence rather than by the consensus of research findings.

The arguments for refining or replacing DRGs with an adjustment for severity of illness stem from a body of research (particularly studies conducted at the Center for Hospital Finance and Management at Johns Hopkins University) indicating that the DRG case mix method has not gone far enough in explaining the costs of inpatient hospital care. These studies reveal wide variations in patients' use of resources within DRGs and show that a severity-of-illness index would account for hospital cost variations better than the DRG method. Various research organizations are addressing such issues as the extent to which some hospitals treat healthier patients within DRG categories, the subjectivity of severity-of-illness classifications, and the feasibility of laying a severity index over the DRG method or altogether replacing DRGs with a severity index.

Expansion Issues. HHS no longer intends to pursue efforts to develop DRGs for physicians' services. Rather, it intends to refine per capita payment systems, which would cover all health care services.

HHS continues to examine the feasibility of developing DRGs for other providers of medical care, including long-term-care facilities, mental health services, and pediatric hospitals. Ten years of DRG development at Yale have shown, however, that breaking down medical care into its component parts is not an easy chore. Nor is attaching equitable reimbursement levels to those components. Thus the government's researchers and their consultants have a full agenda in evaluating the potential for bringing additional groups of providers into a payment per case system.

The states are looking to DRGs as a potential way to contain costs in the Medicaid program. Eight states (New Jersey, Ohio, Pennsylvania, Michigan, Washington, Oregon, Minnesota, and Utah) have already implemented DRG systems for Medicaid; many others, particularly Montana, South Dakota, Texas, Connecticut, West Virginia, and North Carolina, are developing or are committed to DRGs for Medicaid.

If private payers follow governments' lead and reimburse according to DRGs, the effect of PPS will be expanded. Insurance companies that have been unwilling to support the research necessary to reimburse on a per case basis or have been hesitant to be the first payer to rock the system can now piggyback onto a method that, however painstaking to develop, is relatively easy to replicate. Perceptions of how well the current PPS reimbursement scheme is working will have a strong bearing on how widely it is adopted by the private sector.

Efforts by the federal government, state governments, and private payers to expand PPS are indicative of the dominant trend in reimbursement. Payers are adopting a "shape up or ship out" stance with medical providers, and the survival of the high-cost provider is no longer guaranteed. This trend, however, has important implications for hospitals' willingness and ability to provide free care to the medically indigent. As Medicare and all other payers take steps to pay only for the provision of cost-effective care to their own beneficiaries, the cross-subsidization that traditionally finances care for the indigent will disappear. An increasingly important challenge to policy makers (and to researchers) is therefore to promote efficiency in the health care system without driving the poor away from it.

Evaluation Issues. Numerous researchers are interested in measuring the effects and effectiveness of PPS, and there are plenty of issues to keep them occupied. The evaluation effort will cover a broad range of issues, including the following:

• Volume control. Hospitals have incentives under DRGs to admit marginally ill patients and to discharge and readmit patients with multiple problems. Professional review organizations (PROs) are responsible for monitoring admissions and readmissions, and the HCFA has Congress's approval to punish unwarranted increases in admissions.

• Length of stay. Is PPS forcing some Medicare patients out of the hospital too soon and in poorer health than before PPS was implemented? Home health agencies, for example, say they are making more visits to patients and providing more intensive medical care. Hospitals' strong incentives to shorten the length of stay have cost and quality implications, creating a need for research that tracks patients to discover what kinds of patients are receiving earlier discharge, the settings and cost of health care services for these patients after discharge, and their health status.

• DRG creep. Hospitals can achieve higher payments by overstating a patient's diagnosis. To what extent will the incidence of high-cost illnesses artificially creep upward?

• Specialization. Is case mix changing *within* hospitals to reflect those DRGs that an institution handles most profitably? Will this make access difficult for patients with certain illnesses? Does specialization improve the quality of care?

• Substitution. Are services previously delivered in hospitals being relocated to less regulated environments? What effect does this have on overall health care costs?

• Medical technology. To what extent is cost-reducing technology being developed in response to new incentives? Are high-cost technological innovations being implemented or ignored? How have hospitals changed their equipment purchasing practices? Is expensive equipment being shared?

• Physicians' behavior. In what ways are hospitals trying to change their physicians' practice patterns? What has been the physicians' response?

31

The greatest challenge to those evaluating PPS will be to isolate the effects of PPS from all the other dynamics now occurring in the health care system. Although PPS is being sold as a system that will make the government's job easier, it was nevertheless a heavy dose of regulation injected into an already complex and rapidly changing health care system. In addition, because PPS is being phased in, for the next three years two complex regulatory systems with differing incentives will be in effect simultaneously. This situation, though easing the transition to DRGs for hospitals, will not diminish the task researchers face in evaluating PPS.

Conclusions

If the development of PPS is indicative of the relations between researchers and policy makers, the willingness of the politicians both to solicit and to act on the advice of researchers is an encouraging sign. Although PPS may have been a typical case of policy makers' willingness to seek the assistance of researchers, Congress's swift action based on this research was, by all accounts, unusual.

More typically a political struggle would have characterized such a dramatic policy change. Interest groups generally exert at least as much influence as researchers on the policy-making process. Because it is difficult for policy makers to enact changes that are detrimental to any of their constituents, change occurs slowly, if at all. A long list of issues can be cited on which extensive research is undertaken at the request of policy makers who then become unwilling or unable, because of political concerns, to translate the findings into policy changes.

Despite the ease with which PPS passed through the political process, it is now the incumbent policy in a process that favors incremental adjustments over wholesale change. We can thus expect DRGs to remain in effect for a fairly long time, with researchers playing a significant role in the future of the program by performing their usual functions: evaluating the program's effectiveness, identifying its shortcomings, shaping refinements, and developing alternative policies.

Notes

1. Tightening the limits gave hospitals some incentive to economize in the treatment of Medicare beneficiaries, but an inefficient hospital could get around the constraints by shifting to private payers any portion of its costs not paid by Medicare.

2. In response to the Carter administration's hospital cost containment bill

in 1978, Senator Herman Talmadge sponsored a measure setting limits (for both Medicare and Medicaid) according to various classifications of hospitals. The Talmadge bill, which was not enacted, contained provisions for incentive payments to hospitals that held their charges below the limits.

3. The market basket method of adjusting hospital reimbursement was an outgrowth of earlier research conducted to develop an overall inflation adjustment for the economy.

4. Julian Pettengill and James Vertrees, "Reliability and Validity in Hospital Case-Mix Measurement," *Health Care Financing Review* (December 1982), p. 124.

5. A direct teaching adjustment, which is not applied to the DRG rate, is made for the salaries of residents and interns. A second, "indirect" adjustment is also made that, according to the enacting legislation, "is only a proxy to account for a number of factors which may legitimately increase costs in teaching hospitals." The indirect adjustment is applied to the DRG rate—for each 0.1 increase in a hospital's residents-bed ratio, its DRG payments increase by 11.59 percent. Additional research on hospitals' medical education costs suggests that this adjustment overcompensates teaching hospitals. See Anderson and Lave, *Inquiry* (Summer 1986), forthcoming.

3
Health Services Research and the Policy-making Process: State Response to Federal Cutbacks in Programs Affecting Child Health

Ira Moscovice

The Debate over the Relevance of Health Services Research

During the past three decades, as health services research has evolved into a distinct field of investigation, increased concern has been expressed about its relevance to the needs of decision makers and those responsible for formulating public policy.[1] Advocates cite the recent development of the DRG system as an example of the importance of such research to public policy makers. Opponents claim that most health services research focuses on the wrong issues, at the wrong time, and for the wrong decision makers.

This debate highlights three important considerations related to the relevance of health services research. First, its utility would be enhanced by early identification of emerging or future issues amenable to research. Retrospective evaluations of existing programs lend themselves more to rationalizing current policies than to influencing the formulation of policy. Second, the relevance of research is often determined by trade-offs between policy makers' needs for timely information on which to base their decisions and researchers' needs for adequate time to conduct appropriate studies. Third, researchers need to work closely with decision makers to gain a better under-

This paper is based on work supported by a grant from the Northwest Area Foundation and grant number HS 04986 from the National Center for Health Services Research, Office of the Assistant Secretary for Health. I would like to acknowledge the efforts of my colleagues William Craig, Gestur Davidson, Laura Pitt, Cynthia Polich, and Janet Shapiro, which facilitated completion of this work and preparation of this paper.

standing of political constraints. The information a research project generates is rarely the sole factor that dictates the political outcome of important health issues. Researchers should work closely with decision makers to assess the degree of control they exert, the data they need, and how those data will be used to influence the final decision.

The relevant issue is not whether health services research has affected the formulation of health policy but how it can be made more useful to policy makers.[2] Researchers need to learn more about the conditions that stimulate the effective use of research in the making of policy. This paper examines the use of health services research by states in formulating policies to respond to federal cutbacks in child health programs, using Minnesota as an example.

Federal Cutbacks in Programs Affecting Child Health

The federal government has significantly cut back categorical and entitlement programs affecting children and their families. Tables 3–1 and 3–2 summarize these cutbacks, whose extent is further illustrated by the following data.[3]

• During 1982–1983 all states tightened eligibility requirements or reduced services provided by the Medicaid program to mothers and children.

• Between 1979 and 1982 the number of children eligible for Medicaid decreased by 2.5 million while the number of children in poor families increased by 2.7 million.

• Almost 6 million children live in families that have incomes below the poverty line but are not covered by Medicaid.

• Each year approximately 250,000 pregnant women with incomes below the poverty line are not covered for maternity services under Medicaid.

• In 1982 cutbacks were made in services or eligibility in maternal and child health (MCH) block grant programs in forty-seven states.

• In 1982–1983 more than 200,000 children and mothers lost preventive MCH services.[4]

Even though children account for a small proportion of federal health expenditures, tables 3–1 and 3–2 underline the complexity and diversity of federal funding for child health programs.[5] The effect of the funding reductions varies dramatically among states according to the scope of the state Medicaid program, the creativity and flexibility the state exhibits in the use of MCH and other block grant funds, the state's fiscal climate, and private sector initiatives. Using Minnesota as an example, I will examine the role of health services research in

TABLE 3–1

CATEGORICAL CHILDREN'S PROGRAMS, FISCAL YEARS 1982–1984

(millions of dollars)

Program	1982 Current Policy	1983 Budget Proposal	1983 Enacted Level	1984 Budget Proposal	Change 1983–1984 (percent)	Change 1982– 1984 (percent)
Maternal and child health	494.6	347.5	373.0	373.0	0.0	−24.6
Preventive health block grant	107.4	81.6	86.3	85.3	−1.2	−20.6
Mental health block grant	585.8	432.0	439.0	439.0	0.0	−25.1
Development disabilities	64.2	41.7	60.5	41.3	−31.7	−35.7
Immunization	32.9	28.9	39.3	41.9	6.6	27.4
Venereal disease prevention	51.6	45.6	47.7	48.5	1.7	−6.0
Community health centers	350.5	—	295.0	—		
Black lung clinics	4.9	—	3.1	—		
Migrant health	46.8	—	38.1	—		
Family planning	175.1	—	124.1	—		
Primary care research and demonstration	10.8	—	0.0	—		
Adolescent family life	—	16.0	13.6	16.3	19.9	—
Total	1,924.6	1,410.1	1,519.7	1,505.6	−0.9	−21.8

SOURCE: Children's Defense Fund, *A Children's Defense Budget: An Analysis of the President's FY 1984 Budget and Children*, pt. 4, appendixes (Washington, D.C., 1983).

assessing the effects of federal cutbacks on child health and helping the state government to formulate a response to those reductions.

The Impact of Federal Cutbacks on Child Health in Minnesota

Minnesota has historically emphasized its responsibility for meeting its citizens' basic needs. The recent funding cutbacks for services provided through MCH block grant funds and the Medicaid program have caused special concern.

TABLE 3-2

Entitlement Programs of Critical Importance to Children and Families, Fiscal Years 1982–1984

(millions of dollars)

Program	Current Policy before Cuts in Effect for 1984	Reductions in Effect from Cuts in 1982	Reductions in Effect from Cuts in 1983	Current Policy for 1984 after Enacted Reductions	Proposed 1984 Budget	Change 1983–1984 (percent)	Change 1982–1984 (percent)
Food stamps	13,696.0	575.0	625.0	12,496.0	11,739.0	−6.1	−14.3
School lunch	3,271.8	933.0	0.0	2,338.8	2,280.3	−2.5	−30.3
AFDC and child support	9,918.0	1,419.0	236.0	8,263.0	7,531.0	−8.9	−24.1
Foster care	490.2	0.0	0.0	490.2	440.2	−10.2	−10.2
Medicaid	22,714.0	1,292.0	330.0	21,092.0	20,799.0	−1.4	−8.4
Total	50,090.0	4,219.0	1,191.0	44,680.0	42,789.5	−4.2	−14.6

Source: Children's Defense Fund, *Children's Defense Budget.*

MCH Block Grants. The MCH block grant is a key element in the delivery of preventive and health promotion services to mothers and children. The block grant consolidates programs formerly funded under Title V of the Social Security Act, with the addition of programs for sudden infant death, the prevention of lead-based-paint poisoning, hemophilia treatment, Supplemental Security Income (SSI) for disabled children, adolescent pregnancy, and genetic disease.

Block grants have led to greater state and local discretion in decisions on spending the reduced federal funds. Table 3–1 shows a 25 percent reduction in total MCH funds from FY 1982 to FY 1984. These cutbacks, coupled with an insufficient transition period for the shift from categorical to block grant funding, have left gaps in the provision of health and social services to low-income mothers and children.

In addition, state reporting requirements for programs funded through the block grants have been reduced.[6] Consequently, the ability to collect aggregate statistical data on how funding cutbacks have affected the health of children in the United States has essentially been eliminated. This has increased the need for local analyses of the health status of children and mothers in low-income families and their use of health and social services.

In Minnesota the MCH block grant is allocated under the direction of the state Department of Health. The funding for the grant was approximately $7.5 million in FY 1981 and $6.2 million in FY 1984—a 17.3 percent reduction in federal funds to the state, unadjusted for inflation.

The Minnesota legislature established an MCH Advisory Task Force to facilitate planning and to make recommendations to the commissioner of health on the award, distribution, and administration of MCH block grant funds after July 1, 1983. The task force recommended redistributing funds, with special emphasis on identifying and funneling resources to populations at high risk for poor health, in preference to across-the-board or pro rata reductions of funds.

The task force deliberations and recommendations underscore the need for useful local data on the effects of the federal cutbacks. It is difficult to recommend and implement the targeting of funds to those most at risk without this information. When funds are limited, policy makers need local data to determine whether such an approach is more efficient than pro rata reductions.

Medicaid Program. A second area of concern has been the effect of funding reductions on the Medicaid program. Medicaid is a federal-state program that provides medical, hospital, nursing home, and related services to the indigent. In FY 1982 approximately 48 percent of Minnesota's Medicaid beneficiaries were children, but less than 15 percent of Medicaid expenditures were for children—an annual average expenditure of $530 per child.[7]

Although Medicaid is the primary health care financing program for the poor in America, it has never covered most of their health care needs. It has been estimated that Medicaid reaches only 40 percent of children living in poverty.[8] Major gaps in Medicaid coverage of children and women of childbearing age have occurred for two major reasons.

First, Medicaid eligibility for many children has been directly linked to the categorical eligibility requirements of Aid to Families with Dependent Children (AFDC). Many children in intact two-parent families or in families with single female heads with incomes at or near minimum wage levels were not eligible for Medicaid. The categorical link to AFDC has been a major structural obstacle to expanding Medicaid coverage.

Second, state income standards used to determine eligibility for Medicaid are below the federal poverty-level income. Although the standard used to determine Medicaid eligibility for a family of four in Minnesota was the fifth highest in the nation in 1982, it was still well below the federal poverty level.[9] In addition, a smaller proportion of those living in poverty are eligible for Medicaid because state welfare payments have increased in recent years more slowly than the rate of inflation.[10]

Minnesota's Medicaid program is one of the most comprehensive in the country. It offers the complete range of services made optional by the federal government. It provides coverage for two-parent families whose principal wage earners are unemployed and for women who are pregnant for the first time. With congressional passage of the Deficit Reduction Act of 1984 (H.R. 4170), Minnesota now provides Medicaid coverage for virtually all children and pregnant women who are poor enough to receive AFDC but do not meet the categorical eligibility requirements.[11]

One major effect of the federal cutbacks in Minnesota was the loss of Medicaid eligibility by more than 13,500 households during 1982 and 1983 because of the federal Omnibus Budget Reconciliation Act (OBRA) of 1981. OBRA terminated welfare assistance, and hence Medicaid coverage, for the majority of working AFDC recipients and their children.

Critics of the cutbacks predicted many negative consequences of the new regulations, including the inability of those removed from the AFDC program to afford replacement health insurance coverage. This might cause them to delay visits to physicians and dentists, except for acute conditions, and eventually to suffer more severe medical problems. To assess the effects of funding cutbacks on child health, we examined how the loss of Medicaid coverage affected working AFDC recipients in Hennepin County, Minnesota.

In January 1982, 3,326 Hennepin County AFDC recipients, or 22 percent of all recipients in the county, were employed. By the summer of 1982 the AFDC benefits of more than two-thirds of these recipients were terminated because of OBRA. Our research team designed and carried out a longitudinal study of a random sample of families affected by the cuts.[12] We used a quasi-experimental design (a single time series) to assess the effects of OBRA on the health care and health insurance loss of working AFDC recipients. We conducted telephone surveys asking questions about seven major aspects of recipients' lives for the periods immediately preceding implementation of OBRA (January 1982), one year after the cutbacks (January 1983), and two years after the cutbacks (January 1984). The high response rate of 88 percent produced data on 516 families followed from a base-line period before OBRA through the next two years.

The typical survey respondent was a thirty-one-year-old white woman with two children and a high school diploma. At the outset of the study, the majority of respondents worked in clerical or service jobs (such as secretary, file clerk, cashier, or waitress). They received $4 to $6 per hour for a thirty- to forty-hour workweek.

One major concern of state and county administrators was that those whose benefits were terminated would quit their jobs and go back on welfare. This did not happen; less than 13 percent of those removed from the rolls in February 1982 because of OBRA were receiving AFDC benefits two years later. Former recipients who continued working averaged eleven months of work in 1983 and annual gross earnings of $11,487. During the two-year study period the number of hours they worked each week increased from 34.7 to 38.2, their hourly pay rate from $5.45 to $6.58, and the proportion who held second jobs from 4.4 percent to 7.9 percent. This increase in labor force participation more than compensated for the minority of respondents who quit work or reduced their work hours to remain eligible for welfare.

When on AFDC, recipients and their children were covered by Medicaid, although employed recipients often had insurance through their workplaces as well. Eligibility for Medicaid ends when AFDC is terminated, making health care potentially more costly and less accessible.[13] State and local administrators expected that families without adequate health insurance coverage would delay visits to physicians and dentists except for acute conditions.

Most former recipients (95 percent) who continued working had a regular source of health care, 55 percent using a private physician. Almost 40 percent of the respondents and one-fourth of their children had private health insurance coverage (in addition to Medicaid) before the cutbacks. Former recipients who continued to work increased their use of HMOs and decreased their use of private physicians as a usual source of care. They also delayed seeing physicians and dentists because of the cost significantly more often than those who remained on AFDC (38 percent versus 7 percent for delay in seeing physicians and 50 percent versus 10 percent for delay in seeing dentists between August 1983 and January 1984). These recipients reported personally paying 42 percent of their health care bills, or an average monthly out-of-pocket medical expenditure of $42 in January 1984.

Some 16 percent of former recipients who continued working and 28 percent of their children had no health insurance two years after the cutbacks. The percentage without health insurance had decreased, however, from 21 percent of respondents and 35 percent of their children one year after AFDC benefits were terminated.

Children who were off AFDC and without health insurance coverage were more likely to have a single parent who worked fewer hours at a lower wage and earned a lower net income than their counterparts with health insurance coverage. Children without health insurance were less likely to have a usual source of care. They used community clinics, hospital outpatient departments, and emergency rooms more often than children with insurance coverage. They also delayed seeing physicians and dentists because of the cost more frequently than children with insurance (table 3–3).

Only 2 percent of families removed from AFDC and working bought private health insurance directly, because of the cost of obtaining such insurance. The current cost of a typical private health insurance policy for a thirty-year-old woman with two children is approximately $2,000 per year in the Twin Cities area.[14] Those who had private health insurance through their work had considerably weaker coverage than those still on Medicaid, which offers complete coverage for all but one of the optional services.

Children and mothers in low-income families with no or weak health insurance coverage appear to be vulnerable to federal funding cuts. The inability to obtain adequate health care is a significant problem for single-parent households with children (usually headed by a woman) that have been unable to obtain insurance coverage after their AFDC benefits have been terminated.

TABLE 3-3

Significant Differences between Children with and without Health Insurance, January 1984

	Off AFDC, Had Health Insurance	Off AFDC, No Health Insurance	Significance Level (p value)
Average family gross earnings, 1983 (dollars)	11,402	9,445	.001
Average family net income, January 1984 (dollars)	1,274	911	.03
Average number of hours parent worked per week, January 1984	35.1	32.0	.05
Average hourly pay rate for parent, January 1984 (dollars)	6.79	5.93	.001
Families with two parents (%)	22.3	9.4	.01
Had usual source of care, January 1984 (%)	97.8	90.6	.01
Usual source of care, January 1984 (%)			
Community clinic	8.7	21.9	.001
Hospital outpatient department	6.5	9.4	.001
Hospital emergency room	0.8	5.2	.001
Health maintenance organization	29.3	0	.001
Delayed seeing physician because family did not have enough money to pay bill, August 1983–January 1984 (%)	26.8	60.4	.001
Delayed seeing dentist because family did not have enough money to pay bill, August 1983–January 1984 (%)	42.0	63.2	.001

The work on this study continues. We are concentrating on developing and analyzing a multivariate model to assess the relation between health insurance coverage, health status, and other factors and the welfare dependence of those removed from AFDC because of OBRA. The study should give us a better understanding of the importance of health insurance coverage to the work and welfare decisions made by such families.

Responding to Federal Cutbacks in Programs Affecting Child Health

As a follow-up to our study, we are evaluating alternative ways to meet the health needs of low-income children in Minnesota. The Center for Health Services Research held an all-day forum on child health for public and private health providers, state and local policy makers, child health advocates, educators, and insurers. The topics discussed were the current health status of low-income children in Minnesota, the effects of recent federal and state cutbacks on child health, the issue of targeting, and innovative approaches to meeting the unmet health needs of these children.[15] After the forum helped to identify programs that could address those needs, we began to analyze the potential of the programs for successful development and implementation.

The center sponsored a series of meetings with a core group of forum participants to discuss unmet child health needs, to recommend ways of improving the use of existing resources, and to plan programs that would improve the health of these children. Before the meetings a list of programs to consider was circulated. The programs, which would require legislative, programmatic, or organizational changes, included the following:

• improved ways to use schools in the screening, referral, and provision of health services and for health education, which might focus on improving the lifelong health behavior of children
• outreach and early intervention programs to improve risk assessment, referral, and case management for the MCH population; for example, community-based volunteer networks to offer outreach services to high-risk groups, such as single, female heads of households with children and no health insurance
• improved accident prevention programs
• programs to improve the health insurance coverage of all low-income families with children, such as extending Medicaid coverage to the working poor, establishing a risk pool to cover the health costs

43

of the uninsured, or creating incentives for the private sector to improve health insurance coverage for low-wage employees

• the targeting of increased state funds to cost-effective programs that serve low-income children, such as community clinics and other programs that fill the gaps left by the funding cuts

• coordination of public health programs and services statewide, with guidelines and standards that would guarantee a basic core of services for low-income pregnant women and children

• programs to address the health needs of low-income children in outstate Minnesota, which might involve schools, county health departments, community hospitals, and private sector groups

• collection of comprehensive data on the health, use of health services, and needs of low-income children in Minnesota, which could be used to evaluate the effects of new policies (such as capitation) and new programs on these children

Our staff and forum participants identified two of these options as needing further analysis: (1) improving the financing of health services for low-income mothers and children and (2) encouraging healthful behavior in low-income families through the schools.

Health Services Financing Options. The forum and follow-up meetings all pointed to financing of health services as a major problem for low-income families. Although children in families with very low incomes may be eligible for Medicaid, children in families with incomes just above Medicaid eligibility standards often have no health coverage—through either government or private insurance programs.

In 1984 the income limit for Medicaid eligibility was $6,300 for a family of three. Families with incomes above that limit usually cannot afford to pay private insurance premiums. Moreover, many of these families are single-parent households headed by a woman whose job is unlikely to include comprehensive health insurance coverage as a benefit.

Consequently, many of these families "spend down" their resources and become eligible for Medicaid if they have high medical expenses, make use of community clinics that provide low-cost or free care, or do not receive needed services. Two methods of improving coverage for these families were discussed: (1) establishing a statewide insurance risk pool that would finance primary and preventive care for uninsured low-income pregnant women and children under age eighteen and (2) modifying the state Medicaid program to improve coverage for mothers and children.

The initial discussions of the risk pool focused on broadly defining its characteristics. Eligibility for the program might be limited to those with incomes of less than 200 percent of the poverty-level income (approximately $15,000 for a family of four) who were not eligible for Medicaid. Services might be financed through state general revenues, with a sliding fee scale for recipients. The program would not cover major medical expenses (for example, hospitalization) since such large health costs would probably make the family eligible for Medicaid. It would cover routine primary and preventive care for children and pregnant women.

Although this idea appears feasible, a substantial amount of work would be needed to develop it into a legislative proposal. None of the administrative procedures and requirements have been worked out, nor have the likely number of eligible children and women and the resulting costs been estimated. Issues remaining to be addressed include eligibility criteria for clients, coverage, eligibility criteria for providers, cost sharing and copayment mechanisms, selection of fiscal intermediaries, and administrative structure. It seemed prudent to delay further action on this option until the other option was explored further, since expanded coverage for mothers and children under the Medicaid program would affect the scope and cost of the risk pool.

We therefore spent a significant part of our time in exploring ways to take full advantage of the possibilities of the Medicaid program for poor women and children. Alternative ways to modify the state Medicaid program to improve coverage for mothers and children include (1) increasing the income eligibility limits for medical assistance from 100 percent to 133⅓ percent of the state AFDC standard; (2) providing medical assistance to pregnant women aged eighteen to twenty-one who are living with their parents; and (3) extending Medicaid benefits for fifteen months to families who have lost, or will lose, AFDC benefits because of earnings from work.

We pursued the first alternative because of its broad scope and administrative simplicity. This alternative would, for example, raise the income eligibility limit in 1984 for a family of four from $7,345 to $9,793 (table 3–4).

This change is allowable under federal regulations. Eligibility limits can be raised for families and children rather than for the entire Medicaid population (including the aged, blind, and disabled). From a political standpoint, however, it may be necessary to consider those groups as well.

This kind of proposal appears more likely than the risk pool to gain the needed support. Because it would work through an existing program with an established administrative structure, uncertainty about its operation is significantly reduced, estimating its effect on the

TABLE 3–4

INCOME LIMITS FOR MEDICAID, 1984

(dollars)

Household Size	100 Percent of AFDC Standard[a]	133⅓ Percent of AFDC Standard
2	5,191	6,921
3	6,300	8,400
4	7,345	9,793
5	8,253	11,004
6	9,235	12,313

a. Current Medicaid eligibility standard.

intended beneficiaries and its costs is easier, and it would be considerably simpler to set up and market. It would require only revised eligibility standards, whereas the risk pool would require a new administrative structure, eligibility requirements, and intake procedures.

This proposal would preferably be limited to raising the eligibility limits for families and children under eighteen and for pregnant women. Clearly the added expenditures to the state would be considerably less than if all Medicaid recipients were eligible. The following table shows approximately how many more children and pregnant women would be eligible for Medicaid under the increased eligibility standard. (These estimates were derived by the state demographer's office.)

Eligibility Group	Number Now Eligible	Additional Number Eligible at 100–133⅓ Percent of Current Standard
Children under 18	212,000	80,000
Pregnant women	12,000	5,000

The costs of adding Medicaid coverage for the 100–133⅓ percent group can be estimated on the assumptions that (1) that group will have the same monthly rate of eligibility as those now eligible and (2) the annual program cost per client will be the same. Department of Human Services staff members estimated the approximate annual increase in program costs and the state share of those costs. Unfortunately, they were able to do so only for families and children under eighteen because costs per client are not calculated for pregnant women alone. Increasing the eligibility limits for families and children under eighteen would add approximately $40 million to the cost of Medicaid in FY 1986, the state share totaling $16.8 million. This figure does not include funds for outreach activities to encourage eligible people to use the program.

Although everyone involved with this project agreed that improved health care financing for low-income families should be a high priority, this proposal would not be easy to implement. Increasing the Medicaid eligibility limits to 133⅓ percent would require collaboration from many individuals and organizations, including the state legislature, the Minnesota Department of Human Services, the Minnesota Department of Health, the governor's office, child health advocates, and child health providers.

The Medicaid eligibility standard cannot be raised without a change in state law. Although the legislature can make this change alone, it is unlikely to do so without support and possible advocacy from others. The usual procedure for changing existing programs, particularly if the change increases costs, is for the state department responsible to include the change in its budget request. The request is reviewed by the Department of Finance and the governor's office and, if it is approved, is incorporated in proposed legislation.

The proposal to raise income eligibility limits for Medicaid did not have the support of all these groups during the 1985 legislative session. It was not included in the annual budget request from the Department of Human Services. In addition, despite recent improvements in the fiscal status of the state government, legislators and government officials hesitated to introduce new programs that would increase the budget. Those close to the budget process were therefore skeptical that the eligibility limits could be raised in the 1985 session.

Since the proposal was not introduced through the budgetary process, the only option was to introduce it directly. Advocates were able to find a sympathetic legislator to sponsor the proposal. They could not, however, maintain the concerted effort necessary to argue its necessity and merits. In particular, they could not gain the support of the Department of Human Services. The legislature used the surplus that existed in early 1985 to cut taxes significantly and to maintain an adequate budget reserve rather than to appropriate funds for new programs.

Other advocacy groups in Minnesota have been very successful at making gains through the legislative process by meeting with legislators and government officials and by coordinating and orchestrating media coverage and testimony at crucial hearings. Child advocates need to learn from these examples to make the comparable gains that are essential for their constituents. Children have no organized advocacy or lobbying group such as the Minnesota Senior Federation or the Minnesota Association for Retarded Citizens. The advocates tend to be providers of services, who often find it difficult to take time from the day-to-day caring for their constituents to engage in significant lobbying. Without an organized effort, however, children will continue to lose out in the distribution of limited resources.

Health Services Research and Public Policy

Health services research can be relevant to the needs of public policy makers. The Reagan administration is committed to shifting the locus of responsibility for the health and social welfare of our citizens away from the federal government and toward state and local governments. This shift suggests an increased potential for the use of health services research by state and local officials.

Such research should be viewed not as a substitute for the political process but as one of several strategies for implementing that process. The appropriate use of health services research in the formulation of public policy depends on the timeliness and availability of results, the effective dissemination of findings, and the strength of communication channels between the researcher and the policy maker. Researchers must thoroughly understand the policy makers' style as well as political constraints if they want to improve the likelihood that their work will be relevant to policy decisions.

I have described the role of health services research in evaluating the effects of federal cutbacks on child health in Minnesota and assessing potential responses to those cutbacks. These activities are part of a continuing effort at our research center to work on projects that will improve the decision-making abilities of the legislative and executive branches of state government.

When the center began to explore the unmet health needs of low-income children, the response was extremely positive. Many people in the private and public sectors, community clinics or agencies, and the school systems were interested in the problem. Yet it was difficult to find people in the legislature, the governor's office, or the Department of Human Services who were specifically interested.

Child health has recently become of increasing concern to Minnesota's government. This interest deserves encouragement and support. Improving the health of low-income children is a long-term process. The range of alternatives I have described underscores the need for an appropriate combination of strategies. We are beginning to see some changes, including a reexamination of improved Medicaid coverage for these children, the development of innovative programs in the school system, and the recent work of the MCH Advisory Task Force of the state Department of Health. Further support of efforts to address the unmet health needs of the state's low-income children is in the best interests of all Minnesotans.

Notes

1. Institute of Medicine, *Health Services Research* (Washington, D.C.: National Academy of Sciences, 1979); Charles Lewis, "Health Services Research and Innovation in Health Care Delivery: Does Research Make a Difference?" *New England Journal of Medicine*, vol. 297 (1977), pp. 423–27; Statements at NAS Open Meeting, "Status of Health Services Research," *Health Services Research*, vol. 13 (1978), pp. 219–42; and Sherman Williams and Jere Wysong, "Health Services Research and Health Policy Formulation: An Empirical Analysis and a Structural Solution," *Journal of Health Politics, Policy, and Law*, vol. 2 (1977), pp. 362–87.

2. Statements at NAS Open Meeting.

3. Children's Defense Fund, *A Children's Defense Budget: An Analysis of the President's FY 1984 Budget and Children* (Washington, D.C., 1983).

4. Sarah Rosenbaum and Judith Weitz, *Children and Federal Health Care Cuts: A National Survey of the Impact of Federal Health Budget Reductions on State Maternal and Child Health Services during 1982* (Washington, D.C.: Children's Defense Fund, 1983); Karen Davis, Testimony before the U.S. House of Representatives, Committee on Energy and Commerce, Subcommittee on Health and the Environment, Washington, D.C., July 15, 1983; and Children's Defense Fund, *Children's Defense Budget*.

5. Peter Budetti, John Butler, and Peggy McManus, "Federal Health Program Reforms: Implications for Child Health Care," *Milbank Memorial Fund Quarterly*, vol. 60 (1982), pp. 155–81.

6. Mary Peoples and C. Arden Miller, "Monitoring and Assessment in Maternal and Child Health: Recommendations for Action at the State Level," *Journal of Health Politics, Policy, and Law*, vol. 8 (1983), pp. 251–76.

7. George Hoffman, personal communication, 1984.

8. Davis, Testimony.

9. American Public Health Association, *The Child Health Improvement Act of 1983* (Washington, D.C., 1983).

10. Ibid.

11. Judith Weitz and Sarah Rosenbaum, *The Deficit Reduction Act of 1984: Medicaid Changes for Children and Pregnant Women* (Washington, D.C.: Children's Defense Fund, 1984).

12. Ira Moscovice and William Craig, "The Omnibus Budget Reconciliation Act and the Working Poor," *Social Service Review*, vol. 58 (1984), pp. 49–62.

13. A Minnesota federal court decision partially ameliorated this problem by ruling that increased income could not lead to immediate termination of Medicaid coverage. For those removed from AFDC because of increased

earnings, Medicaid eligibility was extended for four months. In addition, the Deficit Reduction Act of 1984 requires states to extend Medicaid coverage for nine months for families removed from AFDC because of earnings from work.

14. The cost was comparable for policies offered by a commercial insurance company (such as Travelers) and by an HMO (such as Group Health).

15. Center for Health Services Research, University of Minnesota, *Innovative Approaches for Addressing the Health Needs of Children in Low-Income Families in Minnesota* (Minneapolis, 1984).

4
Doing Research for Decision Makers: Nursing Home Reimbursement

Barbara Bolling Manard

Nursing home expenditures have grown faster over the past decade than any other separately identified health service in the national income accounts. Approximately 60 percent of those expenditures are public dollars, mostly Medicaid. The growth in expenditures is particularly critical for states, where nursing homes generally account for about half the total Medicaid budget. Concern over these rising costs, predictions of increased demand from an aging population, and consideration for the quality of life and care of the disabled have led to heated debate and to controversial federal and state legislation. The debate focuses primarily on two issues: How should we pay for nursing home care? and Can community-based services such as home care and adult day care serve as cost-effective alternatives to institutionalization?[1] In 1984, for example, twenty-one states had bills pending on nursing home reimbursement and community-based alternatives.[2]

This paper was commissioned as one of a series designed to "describe the role of health services research in the decision-making process and the formulation of public policy"—in this case focused on nursing homes and related policies. A review of the literature on the use of social science research in public policy making reveals two views of the situation. One line of discussion reports that many policy makers are indifferent or even hostile to policy research and that a remarkably large number of the social scientists studied believe that they have something important to say to policy makers but are ignored and that this constitutes a social problem.[3]

Another line of argument, and increasingly of empirical research, suggests that public policy is in fact very much influenced by research but that this influence is difficult to trace.[4] One analyst has suggested that the two opposing diagnoses stem from different definitions of public policy. Those who contend that health services research has little influence on policy typically conceive of public policy as "explicit and authoritative decisions taken by identifiable government officials"; those who see research as influential view formal public policy as an "accretion of decentralized, pluralistic actions and decisions."[5]

The various diagnoses have been accompanied by a sometimes conflicting set of prescriptions for improving the effectiveness or usefulness of health services research. A striking feature of this diagnostic and prescriptive literature is the relative thinness of the descriptive information on which it is built. Few empirical investigations examine how health services research is produced or used; virtually none look at the reimbursement of nursing homes.

The purpose of this paper is to contribute to the empirical base on which analyses of the use of health services research in public decision making must ultimately rest. Specifically, my aim is to describe some of the problems and solutions of researchers who work in nursing home reimbursement and related areas in dealing with three aspects of doing research for policy makers: understanding and working with the constraints of the policy world; choosing a practice environment; and communicating effectively. Each of these has been a focus of prescriptions for improving the use of health services research in public policy.

Understanding the Constraints and Opportunities of the Policy World

With some notable exceptions, most policy researchers working on nursing home reimbursement and related issues were trained in economics, political science, and, to a lesser degree, sociology. The academic traditions of these fields—the reward structures for those who practice in traditional settings—emphasize a search for general principles, reliance on sophisticated, increasingly quantitative methods, publication in peer-reviewed technical journals, and at least the appearance of building cumulatively on previous research and theory. A key determinant of successful research in that context is the certainty, or "truth," of the findings.

In contrast, the policy world requires relevance, timeliness, and answers to specific questions. The emphasis is more on finding a "not too badly wrong" answer right now than on finding a "correct" answer at some later date. At a later date the budget deadline will be passed, the issues will have shifted, and the assistant secretary will have been replaced.

The tension between the perspectives of the researcher and of the policy maker is repeatedly manifest in the push and pull between legislators and the executive branch, between policy analysts and decision makers in both branches, and between program staff and evaluation researchers. As an aide to Boston's Mayor Kevin White remarked, "I'm an academic by background, but my hostility to academics grew fast when I took this job. They came and proposed studies, went away a long time, and then produced something very long. No one read it."[6]

The differences between the culture of research and the realities of the political process are quite real. But emphasis on these differences has sometimes led, in my view, to a false distinction between "good" research (that is, research that meets the most rigorous methodological standards) and "relevant" research. The real issue for policy researchers is matching the scope and design of the research to the subject and to the uses required of the findings. In some situations the only relevant research (that is, research that can have a serious influence on the decision-making process) will be research that employs the most rigorous "scientific" methods. In other cases the process of abstraction required for rigorous "scientific" evaluation of hypotheses may be utterly unsuited to the task at hand. Two examples may illustrate these differences.

A Search for Certainty: Research on Alternatives to Institutionalization. The debates over the past few years about the cost effectiveness of community-based care and the role of researchers in those debates provide one of the better examples of the tension between the time required for research to provide *certain* answers and the far shorter time available for the policy process. In 1972, as part of a complex restructuring of the Social Security Act, Congress authorized waivers of certain Medicare provisions to permit the use of Medicare financing for community, rather than institutional, services in certain defined research demonstration projects.[7] These projects were known as the 222 demonstrations, after the section of the legislation authorizing them. Their purpose was to determine (1) how much it would cost to provide adult day care and homemaker-chore services to Medicare beneficiaries, (2) whether such services would improve the social and physical functioning of frail elderly participants, and (3) whether costs could be reduced by substituting these community services for institutionalization.

In the mid-1970s the National Center for Health Services Research (NCHSR) undertook a sophisticated evaluation project at some of the demonstration sites. Clients were randomly assigned to control and experimental groups and were followed for a year.

53

During the same period the Administration on Aging and the NCHSR funded other studies and demonstrations focusing on alternatives to institutionalization.[8] Although each of these projects had a research and evaluation component, many were viewed and run principally as demonstrations oriented toward the delivery of services. Some who organized and ran the projects became passionate advocates of the home care cause, and a few became effective political forces.[9]

As pressure built on Capitol Hill for expansion of home care, the Department of Health and Human Services (HHS) intensified efforts to find policy answers in the research. Several assessments of the evaluation demonstrations were commissioned; most were highly critical, emphasizing the limits to certainty posed by methodological shortcomings in the research and by the limited amount of research. For example, one reviewer wrote:

> To date, the failure of the long-term care research to provide valid findings on the effectiveness of community-based alternatives to institutionalization for the impaired aged, is directly due to a lack of vigor in the research design. . . . But even had the research been more rigorous we would still have major gaps in our knowledge since (only) a narrow range of options have been tested.[10]

In the summer of 1979 the NCHSR published the first report of the randomized experiment on day care and homemaker-chore services. The author, William Weissert, concluded that "for the majority of patients, day care and homemaker services probably served as additional benefits under Medicare rather than substitutes for nursing home care. Net total Medicare costs were 71 percent higher for the day care experimental group and 60 percent higher for the homemaker experimental group."[11]

These findings ran counter to some strongly held beliefs. When the General Accounting Office (GAO) issued its report to Congress in November 1979 on ways to reduce Medicaid expenditures on nursing homes, it stressed the need for community-based alternatives. The Department of Health and Human Services (then called the Department of Health, Education and Welfare) pointed out in a letter to the GAO that its report failed to take note of the Weissert findings. The GAO responded that it had reviewed those studies carefully but stuck to its conclusion that "most long-term care research and demonstration projects have failed to produce conclusive evidence regarding the effectiveness of these services in reducing avoidable institutionalization because of critical weaknesses in the design and implementation of the research."[12]

By December 1979 the HHS was planning a new set of experiments. This time it was testing the effect of targeting community services to those most at risk of institutionalization and was organizing its third task force in five years to study policy options in long-term care.[13] Among the department's continuing concerns was whether expanded benefits for community services would reduce outlays by reducing reliance on costly nursing homes or simply be an "add-on" service, providing new and costly benefits to a new population. Responsibility for the task force, chaired by the under secretary of HHS, was largely in the hands of John Palmer, an economist from Stanford University and the Brookings Institution.

In hearings held on December 11, 1979, by the Subcommittee on Health of the House Commerce Committee, the chair, Henry Waxman, reflected the apparent impatience of Congress with more studies and task forces: "You keep telling us that you need more information and more studies. We are concerned that sometimes studies are your rationalization for inactivity."

A written exchange between Waxman and the department after the December hearings included the following remarks:

Waxman: Your Department has spent a great deal of time and money on demonstration projects in this area, beginning in the early 70's. I have here reports from some of those projects, from Connecticut, from Georgia. Is none of this information valid? Have we learned nothing on which we can base recommendations? What are you doing to make use of information you have?

HHS: The projects you refer to, Triage, in Connecticut and Alternative Health Services in Georgia, are both in their fourth year of Federal support. Both projects were initally funded by HEW before the establishment of HCFA [Health Care Financing Administration]. . . . We would not be comfortable making recommendations for program change based on preliminary analysis of data, especially from only two projects. . . . The addition of data from the evaluation of projects recently funded will provide us with a firm basis for decision making as these projects mature and data is collected and analyzed.

Waxman: [With regard to the new task force] Have you been in contact with people who served on similar policy groups in the not-so-distant past? Have you asked those people to describe what happened during those well-intentioned attempts? Will you

	find out why previous task-forces failed? You described a new, intra-agency process for "analyzing needs and establishing research priorities." Can you tell us why this process is different from all other previous processes? Who is involved? What are they expected to do?
HHS:	While past activity has yielded some progress, there have been short-comings as well. Each effort has been a temporary, one-time attempt to address a variety of complex issues relating to long-term care. The purpose of this Task Force is to identify those long-term care issues which the Department should address, to make the staff assignments necessary to address these issues, and to propose recommendations to the Secretary with respect to long-term care for the Department.[14]

Despite the appearance of an overcautious bureaucracy and an impatient Congress, Congress was also unwilling to commit itself to potentially costly new benefits without any clear idea of how expenditures could be limited. In 1981 Congress gave the secretary authority to grant waivers to states to allow Medicaid coverage of a broad range of community-based services, including day care and homemaker services. The waivers were to be granted, however, only on the states' assurance that total Medicaid costs would not exceed what they would have been if the beneficiaries had been institutionalized and that persons who received the community services be identifiably at high risk of institutionalization. In brief, a whole new round of experiments, demonstrations, and evaluations was begun.

The controls on expenditures built into the 1981 legislation were partially a function of strong findings from well-designed research and partially a function of changing political and economic realities. By 1985 federal and state concerns about controlling health care expenditures were so great that even "positive" results from the channeling demonstrations seemed unlikely to lead to federal legislation to expand community care benefits beyond experimental demonstrations.

A Search for Sense: The Design of Nursing Home Reimbursement Systems. The way in which policy decisions are made about the design of systems for reimbursing nursing homes contrasts sharply with the demands for certainty in research on the cost effectiveness of community-based care. Medicaid officials in every state design and redesign reimbursement systems quite confidently and sometimes quite wisely despite the absence of even approximately definitive research findings on the effects of various components of such systems.

Nursing home reimbursement systems are generally complex creations, described in thirty or forty pages of detailed rules specifying policy decisions on a myriad of details, including

- whether the rates will be set prospectively or retrospectively
- whether facilities should be grouped by size, ownership, location, or other factors for establishing ceilings
- whether total costs or individual cost centers should be low or high
- what kind of inflation allowances should be used in projecting targets or for setting interim rates in retrospective systems
- whether specific incentives to encourage the admission of patients needing heavy care should be included
- how capital costs should be reimbursed

These fundamental elements and choices were first described by Pollack nearly a decade ago in an essay that analyzed incentives with respect to costs, quality, and access to care.[15]

Most efforts to test propositions about hypothesized workings of nursing home reimbursement systems have been largely unsatisfactory.[16] Part of the problem is the sheer difficulty of getting good data with adequate measures of relevant variables. For example, both the quality of care provided in a nursing home and the severity of the patients' conditions clearly influence the cost of providing care. A definitive study of nursing home reimbursement would require comparable data sets from several states over time and continuing good information on costs (which can, with difficulty, be obtained) and on quality and patients' needs, among other things. Such data sets have not been created. In addition, the usefulness of much of the existing research is severely limited because many researchers' questions about nursing home costs and reimbursement systems simply do not make sense in the context of how policy decisions are actually made.

Researchers have asked, for example, whether prospective or retrospective reimbursement is a more effective device for restraining Medicaid per diem payments. This question has been studied with careful attention to statistical techniques.[17] The answer is that states with prospective systems over the periods studied have experienced slower growth in average per diem rates. Even the greenest Medicaid director, however, can devise ways to make expenditures under a retrospective system grow more slowly than expenditures under a prospective system.

Nursing home reimbursement systems are built incrementally; they are more likely to be changed by tinkering than by wholesale restructuring. Thus policy makers need to know what would happen to nursing home costs or to access for Medicaid patients or to the quality of care if a particular change in a system were made, assuming that the rest of a particular system remained the same. Researchers, however, have rarely approached the issue of nursing home reimbursement from this perspective.

Choosing a Practice Environment

An obvious fact about the policy world is that most of the key decision makers are located in Washington and state capitals. Nevertheless, high-quality research that is useful to policy makers can be and is conducted by people who do not live in those places and who are employed in a variety of settings: academic departments, schools of policy and public health, government agencies, think tanks and institutes, trade associations, and consulting firms. It has been argued that some environments (for example, universities) are better suited to "high-quality" research while others (for example, institutes and consulting firms) are better suited to "relevant" research. I am increasingly less convinced that much truth lies in this particular theory of environmental determinism.

The key to combining quality, relevance, and effectiveness is access to appropriate resources—time, people, and information. This occurs when links are formed between people with the particular skills needed for a particular task. In the area of nursing home reimbursement (and, I suspect, in other policy areas), these people are scattered across the country, work in many different settings, and often move about.

The complexity of the links that are typically formed would make any test of our common assumptions about the "best" environments for policy research difficult (even setting aside the problem of identifying high-quality and effective research). For example, the 222 evaluation associated with Weissert was built on research conducted at TransCentury, a for-profit consulting firm. It depended on data collected by another consulting firm under contract to the federal government and was guided by an advisory committee that included luminaries from academia and other settings. Its results were originally reported by Weissert during his tenure as a federal employee. The evaluation has continued to spin off analyses and reanalyses by people in many different settings as well as by Weissert himself, who subsequently moved from the government to the Urban Institute and is now at the University of North Carolina.

58

Access to appropriate information, more than access to skills, may be determined in part by the environment and location of a researcher. University libraries rarely contain the documents, unpublished reports, memorandums, and papers that form the core of the "literature" in policy research. Two bibliographies on nursing home reimbursement illustrate the dependence of that field of policy research on unpublished literature.

In 1975 the NCHSR engaged a consulting firm to compile a comprehensive bibliography of research on nursing home reimbursement.[18] The search produced a list of 108 items; forty-four were on nursing homes and the rest on related topics; only four works directly related to the topic had been published in books or journals. Six years later the NCHSR sponsored another literature search on nursing home reimbursement.[19] The resulting bibliography contained 111 items directly related to the subject—more than twice the number found in the earlier search. This increase reflects not only the development of the field but also the importance of unpublished works. More than half (63 percent) of the items are conference papers, state reports, and reports prepared by government contractors.

The findings of some government-sponsored research projects are eventually published as books or in journals (the Health Care Financing Administration increasingly encourages and in some cases requires this). But the lag time for publication in most journals, as well as the lack of time (or interest) many policy researchers have for preparing journal articles, means that current research findings tend to have limited circulation. A variety of sponsoring agencies are concerned about this issue from the standpoint of the cost effectiveness of publicly sponsored research. Others are concerned about the quality control of a literature that is for the most part not subject to the normal peer review process. For the policy researcher, however, failure to gain access to the unpublished literature or to the people who produce it can mean critical isolation from emerging definitions of the issues. It is that isolation, I think, that makes it difficult for many researchers to participate effectively in the policy process.

Communicating Effectively

Common sense, as well as a cursory glance at academic journals and technical reports, indicates that many researchers need to learn how to

- write clearly
- write briefly
- write summaries

Communicating research to policy makers effectively, however, is not a matter of reporting one's results through the *American Journal of Public Health* in the bulleted form (illustrated above) peculiar to policy memos and briefing papers. Most decision makers do not read the journal, and neither do their staffs. Research findings appear to reach policy makers directly through phone calls, briefings, workshops, and hearings and indirectly through analytic papers, syntheses, and briefing papers.

Virtually all prescriptions for improving the effectiveness of health services research call for more attention to presenting results clearly and to dissemination.[20] Both prescriptions have consequences for the research community that bear closer scrutiny. First, clarity of communication requires simplification, and simplification virtually always entails value choices. The prescription to be clear and effective may, in many instances, conflict with the prescription to be objective and mindful of the limitations of one's work. Second, dissemination occurs through repetition. But repetition and dissemination may operate like gossip—the more often studies are cited and discussed, the more the findings are subtly—and not so subtly—shaded and reshaped.

Clarity and Values: Researchers in Direct Contact with Policy Makers. Jay Greenberg of Brandeis University, an experienced policy researcher in long-term care, describes the researchers' dilemma in direct communication with policy makers: "You can keep your researchers' hat on and be safe by emphasizing the unknowns and the complexities (on the one hand this, on the other hand that). In this case, you will bore them, and not be helpful. Alternatively, you can be more definite about conclusions and policy implications, but risk giving bad advice."[21] Similarly, Bill Weissert attributes the impact of his 222 experiments in part to the definiteness of his stated conclusions, although others have criticized him for having "oversold" the results. Striking an appropriate balance between effective communication and research integrity is a critical and acquired skill.

Figure 4–1 reproduces two slides that were part of an interim briefing given to Minnesota officials. They illustrate both successful simplification and the difficulty of balancing a desire to be effective and maintenance of the researchers' perspective. The purpose of the Minnesota project was to help the state develop a new reimbursement system for nursing homes, taking into account variations among nursing homes in the condition of the patients they serve (that is, the case mix).

The particular briefing for which the slides were prepared was

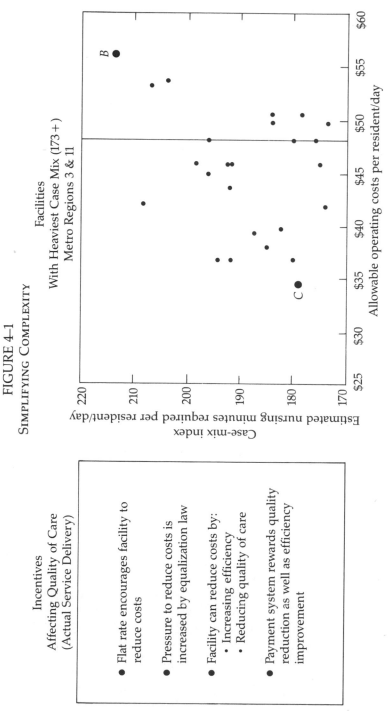

FIGURE 4–1
SIMPLIFYING COMPLEXITY

Incentives
Affecting Quality of Care
(Actual Service Delivery)

● Flat rate encourages facility to reduce costs

● Pressure to reduce costs is increased by equalization law

● Facility can reduce costs by:
  • Increasing efficiency
  • Reducing quality of care

● Payment system rewards quality reduction as well as efficiency improvement

Facilities
With Heaviest Case Mix (173 +)
Metro Regions 3 & 11

Case-mix index
Estimated nursing minutes required per resident/day

Allowable operating costs per resident/day

SOURCE: Barbara Manard, Judy Feder, and William Scanlon, *Minnesota Case-Mix Reimbursement Study*, Presentation to Interagency Board, January 1984.

designed to help officials decide on the broad outlines of a revised payment system. A key issue was whether the state should pay the same rate to all nursing homes in the same geographic area and with the same case mix. Paying a flat rate, as it is called, means that facilities with costs above the rate must reduce expenditures while those with costs below the rate get to keep the difference as profit. The facilities appear to have clear economic incentives to reduce expenditures. As the first slide shows, however, facilities can reduce costs by increasing efficiency or reducing the quality of care or both. Creating strong incentives to reduce expenditures may also create incentives to reduce quality. The first slide brings to the policy-making process a four-bullet summary of analytical thought and research on incentives in nursing home reimbursement with a ten-year history of debate and a very limited amount of empirical testing. To what extent would facilities reduce expenditures below the rate to make a profit? In doing so, how many facilities would reduce quality rather than increase efficiency? Research does not have an answer. Should the first bullet have read, "There is very little empirical research on this topic"? Would it have made a difference to the policy makers' understanding or choices?[22]

Choosing which information to eliminate for the sake of simplicity requires judgments about the basis on which decisions will, and to some degree should, be made. "Should" questions are value questions; hence the act of simplifying always blurs the distinction between the objective researcher and the political process.

The second slide illustrates a flat rate system, based on reports on costs from Minnesota facilities. The vertical line represents a rate set at the sixtieth percentile of costs among facilities. Each dot represents one facility. Like many pictures, this was particularly effective. One point the picture conveyed was that, with the reimbursement rate set at $48 per day, facility C, with a relatively light case mix, would realize a $13 per day profit—the difference between its costs and the rate. Facility B, with a heavier case mix, would experience about an $8 per day shortfall.

The clearest, most direct way of describing the implications or meaning of the difference between facility C's costs and the rate is to call it a windfall profit. This is a term that has immediate impact: it is memorable. It is also value laden (which is why it is memorable). We used the term "windfall profit" in a legislative hearing and were challenged by an industry representative. Were we being clear and effective? Or seemingly biased and hence ineffective?

Indirect Communication: Dissemination and the Reshaping of Research Results. One way for researchers to disseminate their results is to write and speak plainly and often on the same topic in many forums. Mark Meiners's research on long-term-care insurance, for which he is widely known, was first presented at a meeting of the American Public Health Association, then in a trade association journal with wide circulation among providers if not academics, then again in the Washington policy journal *Health Affairs;* finally it was reprinted for distribution by his employer, the NCHSR.[23]

For a variety of reasons, however, research is likely to be disseminated to the policy community through "bridging" documents: policy analyses, syntheses, and reviews.[24] The role of these documents in shaping interpretations of research deserves better study. For Weissert's 222 experiments, for example, a clear pattern can be seen. Virtually all of the numerous policy analyses and syntheses of research that mention this study in time accepted (that is, repeated accurately) the key finding regarding cost: the community-based services studied were an "add-on," unlikely to prevent institutionalization, at least in the form studied. In time, however, while Weissert's own reconsideration of these results led to stronger conclusions about the lack of any significant benefit, the ideology emerging from the policy analyses and syntheses was that while the costs may be an add-on, benefits may offset this.

The original study summarizes the findings in a two-page, carefully worded, bulleted format. Seven outcomes are discussed with respect to two services. The effects of day care and homemaker services are modest, somewhat confusing, and sufficiently complicated to allow various interpretations, a sample of which follow.

> Both the Section 222 and the one year BRI experiments, however, did indicate positive impacts of services on contentment levels of service recipients. Moreover, the Section 222 experiments showed improved levels of mental functioning and social activity.[25]

> There is very little research which evaluates the effect of . . . day care on the quality of the client's life. The limited research that exists [the synthesis relied on Weissert's work and a report from Connecticut] has reported these positive impacts of day care programs:
> - Improved physical functioning . . .
> - Improved levels of contentment . . .
> - Decreased mortality . . .[26]

> Weissert found home services to be an addition to, not a substitute for, existing Medicare SNF (post hospital) benefits and that costs were $3,442 per year higher for experimentals than controls. The social and mental functioning of recipients was unaffected although contentment increased. The

63

provision of day care reduced the use of both SNFs and hospitals. Death rates were reduced slightly but dependency, contentment, and mental and social functioning were only minimally affected.[27]

Weissert also reported better functional levels in the day care experimental group as compared to the controls, *but* the difference between these two groups diminished over the evaluation year, making it uncertain if they would persist in an on-going program. In general, no project could document that its intervention produced statistically significant differences between the experimental and control groups in client functional ability.[28]

[With regard to adult day care] Patient outcomes, as measured by change in functional ability to perform activities of daily living, were significantly better for the day care group.

Outcomes in contentment, mental functioning, and social activity were not significantly different between the two groups.[29]

Interestingly, for the smaller experimental group receiving both day care and homemaker services, costs were only 38 percent higher than for the control group. However, a significantly higher portion of the patients receiving the combined services either improved or maintained their level of contentment, mental functioning ability and social activity, compared to those in the control group.

Although the importance of cost cannot be overlooked, it is equally important to consider the intangible benefits community-based services bring to an elderly person. The issue to be resolved now is whether society should consider cost alone in evaluating community-based programs, or whether the value of lower mortality, better social functioning, higher contentment, and the ability to function independently and with dignity outweighs the benefits of reduced expenditures.[30]

The emerging consensus about what the Weissert studies say to policy makers is captured best in the unmatchably descriptive title of the most recent GAO report on the topic: "The Elderly Should Benefit from Expanded Home Health Care, but Increasing These Services Will Not Insure Cost Reductions."[31]

Agenda for the Future

I am well aware of the problems associated with an anecdotal approach to research and analysis. But we as health services researchers need to devote much more effort to describing exactly what we do before we take our own diagnoses and prescriptions for reform too seriously. Particularly sobering is Lindbloom's reminder that much of what we do is not derived from a specialized way of seeing or knowing but relies "heavily on the same ordinary techniques of speculation, definition, conceptualization, hypothesis formulation, verification as are practiced by persons who are not social scientists or professional investigators of any kind."[32]

That observation and the very difficult problems of dealing honestly with values and facts in policy research lead me to a final observation—a prescription, of course, for improving health policy research. We need to apply to our research a rigorous self-awareness as well as a rigorous attention to its professional qualities. This conference with its attention to case studies and real-world examples is an excellent effort in that direction.

Notes

1. A third set of issues concerns the role of government regulation, inspection, and standards in the quality of care.

2. Barbara Yondorf and Ellen Hekman, *Major Health Issues for the States: 1984,* Health Care Cost Containment Paper no. 2 (Denver: National Conference of State Legislators, 1984).

3. See, in particular, the essays and reports in Carol Weiss, *Using Social Research for Public Policy Making* (Lexington, Mass.: D. C. Heath and Company, 1977).

4. Cf. Stephen Shortell and James P. LoGerfo, "Health Services Research and Public Policy: Definitions, Accomplishments, and Potential," *Health Services Research* (Fall 1978), pp. 230–38.

5. Thomas W. Bice, "Social Science and Health Services Research: Contributions to Public Policy," *Milbank Memorial Fund Quarterly,* vol. 58 (Spring 1980), pp. 173–200.

6. Cited in Peter Szanton, *Not Well Advised* (New York: Russell Sage Foundation, 1981).

7. The law (P.L. 92–603) grew out of Richard Nixon's comprehensive welfare reform bill and eventually included nineteen provisions related to nursing homes—largely reflecting efforts to address problems of quality identified during a lengthy set of hearings conducted by the Senate Long-Term Care Subcommittee. For a history of the issues, see Bruce C. Vladeck, *Unloving Care: The Nursing Home Tragedy* (New York: Basic Books, 1980).

8. The increasing emphasis on long-term-care issues was spurred in part by continuing exposés of nursing home quality and financing—notably the work of the New York Moreland Act Commission. Policy makers' interest did not go unnoticed by funding agencies. The first major study of nursing homes in which I was involved was funded by the Administration on Aging in 1972—two years after the proposal had been "accepted but not funded."

9. A review of projects in 1977, for example, noted with regard to a Connecticut project:

This project has had a long and turbulent history and has been highly politicized. Waivers were authorized under P.L. 92-603, Section 222(b), to allow all service costs, estimated to be approximately five million dollars, to be paid out of the Medicare Trust Fund. The service component of the project has reportedly been functioning well. The major problems have occurred with the evaluation component. Despite repeated disapprovals of the design by the official review panel, funding was mandated from the top of the Department with the requirement that an acceptable design be worked out. At the time of [this] review, negotiations were in progress.

Sonia Conley, *Critical Review of Research on Long-Term Care Alternatives* (Prepared for the Department of Health, Education and Welfare, Office of the Assistant Secretary for Planning and Evaluation), June 1977.

10. Ibid.

11. National Center for Health Services Research, *Effects and Costs of Day Care and Homemaker Services for the Chronically Ill: A Randomized Experiment*, DHEW Publication no. PHS 79-3250, August 1979.

12. U.S. General Accounting Office, *Entering a Nursing Home—Costly Implications for Medicaid and the Elderly*, PAD-80-12, November 26, 1979.

13. The channeling projects are the major component of a multisite demonstration and randomized experiment, originally estimated to cost $20 million. "Channeling," which means "case management," is a term deemed to convey a less authoritarian view of the relation between an elderly client and the person who helps link the client with appropriate services.

14. For a variety of reasons, the task force ultimately made no policy recommendations in its final report, completed in the eleventh hour of the Carter administration.

15. William Pollack, "Long Term Care Facility Reimbursement," in John Holahan et al., *Altering Medicaid Provider Reimbursement Methods* (Washington, D.C.: Urban Institute, 1977).

16. Notable exceptions include the work of William Scanlon, Judith Feder, and their colleagues. See, for example, Judith Feder and John Holahan, *Financing Health Care for the Elderly* (Washington, D.C.: Urban Institute, 1979); Judith Feder and William Scanlon, "Regulating the Bed Supply in Nursing Homes," *Milbank Memorial Fund Quarterly*, vol. 58 (Winter 1980), pp. 54–88; and Holahan et al. *Altering Medicaid Provider Reimbursement Methods.*

17. James H. Swan and Charlene Harrington, "Medicaid Reimbursement Systems and Rates for Nursing Homes: Effects on Utilization and Expenditures" (Paper presented at the 192d meeting of the American Public Health Care Association, 1984).

18. Applied Management Science, *Report on Systems of Reimbursement for Long-Term Care Services* (Prepared for the National Center for Health Services Research, contract no. HRA 106-74-186), 1975.

19. Eileen Tynan, Daniel Holub, and Robert Schlenker, *A Synthesis of Research on Nursing Home Reimbursement* (Prepared for the National Center for Health Services Research, contract no. 233-79-3025), 1981.

20. Stephen Shortell and Marian A. Solomon, "Improving Health Care

Policy Research," *Journal of Health Politics, Policy, and Law*, vol. 6 (Winter 1982), pp. 684–702; Bice, "Social Science and Health Services Research"; and Herbert E. Klarman, "Observations on Health Services Research and Health Policy Analysis," *Milbank Memorial Fund Quarterly*, vol. 58 (Spring 1980), pp. 201–15.

21. Jay Greenberg, personal communication.

22. The discussion included lively exchanges between the decision makers and the analysts about the limits of certainty with regard to research on flat rates. But the "simple" chart remains as the record.

23. Mark Meiners, "The Case for Long-Term Care Insurance," *Health Affairs*, vol. 2 (Summer 1983); and Meiners, *The Case for Long-Term Care Insurance*, National Center for Health Services Research reprint, 1983-381-787, p. 316.

24. Peter Fox, former director of the HCFA's Office of Policy Analysis, attributes the need for bridging documents between the researcher and the policy maker to the following circumstances: researchers do not always draw the best or most appropriate policy implications from their work; policy makers need to know what the weight of the evidence says, rather than a litany of research results; and policy makers' staffs know how much information in what form is best presented to a particular policy maker. Fox, personal communication.

25. Burton D. Dunlop, "Expanded Home-based Care for the Impaired Elderly: Solution or Pipe Dream?" *American Journal of Public Health*, vol. 70 (May 1980), pp. 514–19.

26. Paula Steiner and Jack Needleman, *Cost Containment in Long Term Care: Options and Issues in State Program Design* (Prepared for the National Center for Health Services Research), 1981.

27. Department of Health and Human Services, Office of the Assistant Secretary for Planning and Evaluation, *Working Papers on Long-Term Care*, 1981.

28. Health Care Financing Administration, *Long Term Care: Background and Future Directions*, 1981.

29. Bettina Kurowski and Linda Breed, *A Synthesis of Research on Client Needs Assessment and Quality Assurance Programs in Long-Term Care* (Prepared for the National Center for Health Services Research, contract no. 233-79-3025), 1981.

30. Gail Toff, *Alternatives to Institutional Care for the Elderly: An Analysis of State Initiatives* (Washington, D.C.: Intergovernmental Health Policy Project, 1981).

31. General Accounting Office, "The Elderly Should Benefit from Expanded Home Health Care, but Increasing These Services Will Not Insure Cost Reductions," 1982.

32. Charles E. Lindbloom and David K. Cohen, *Usable Knowledge: Social Science and Problem Solving* (New Haven, Conn.: Yale University Press, 1979).

Bibliography

Applied Management Science. *Report on Systems of Reimbursement for Long-Term Care Services.* Prepared for the National Center for Health Services Research (Contract no. HRA 106-74-186), 1975.

Bice, Thomas W. "Social Science and Health Services Research: Contributions to Public Policy." *Milbank Memorial Fund Quarterly* 58 (Spring 1980):173–200.

Conley, Sonia. *Critical Review of Research on Long-Term Care Alternatives.* Prepared for Department of Health, Education and Welfare, Office of the Assistant Secretary for Planning and Evaluation, 1977.

Dunlop, Burton D. "Expanded Home-based Care for the Impaired Elderly: Solution or Pipe Dream?" *American Journal of Public Health* 70 (May 1980):514–19.

Estes, Carroll L., Philip R. Lee, Charlene Harrington, Robert Newcomer, Lenore Gerard, Mary Kreger, A. E. Benjamin, and James Swen. *Long Term Care for California's Elderly: Policies to Deal with a Costly Dilemma.* Berkeley: University of California, Institute of Governmental Studies, 1981.

Feder, Judith, and John Holahan. *Financing Health Care for the Elderly.* Washington, D.C.: Urban Institute, 1979.

Feder, Judith, and William Scanlon. "Regulating the Bed Supply in Nursing Homes." *Milbank Memorial Fund Quarterly* 58 (Winter 1980): 54–88.

Greenberg, Jay. "The Cost of In-Home Services." In *A Planning Study of Services to Noninstitutionalized Older People in Minnesota,* edited by N. Anderson. Minneapolis: Governor's Citizens Council on Aging, 1974.

Greenberg, Jay, Martha Schmitz, and K. Charlie Lakin. *An Analysis of Responses to the Medicaid Home and Community-based Long-Term Care Waiver Program.* Prepared for the State Medicaid Information Center, National Governors' Association, 1983.

Grimaldi, Paul L. *Medicaid Reimbursement of Nursing-Home Care.* Washington, D.C.: American Enterprise Institute, 1982.

Holahan, John F. *Financing Health Care for the Poor: The Medicaid Experience.* Washington, D.C.: Urban Institute, 1974.

Holahan, John, and Joel Cohen. "Reimbursing Nursing Homes." In *New Approaches to the Medicaid Crisis,* edited by Robert Blendon and Thomas W. Moloney. New York: F & S Press, 1982.

Holahan, John, Bruce Spitz, William Pollack, and Judith Feder. *Altering Medicaid Provider Reimbursement Methods.* Washington, D.C.: Urban Institute, 1977.

Karpoff, Peter. "A Proposal for Reforming Nursing Home Reimbursement under Medicaid." Ph.D. dissertation, University of Wisconsin, 1971.

Klarman, Herbert E. "Observations on Health Services Research and Health Policy Analysis." *Milbank Memorial Fund Quarterly* 58 (Spring 1980):201–15.

Kurowski, Bettina, and Linda Breed. *A Synthesis of Research on Client Needs Assessment and Quality Assurance Programs in Long-Term Care.* Prepared for the National Center for Health Services Research (Contract no. 233-79-3025), 1981.

Lindbloom, Charles E., and David K. Cohen. *Usable Knowledge: Social Science and Problem Solving.* New Haven, Conn.: Yale University Press, 1979.

Malone, Joelyn K. "Reimbursement of Nursing Staff Resources in Minnesota Nursing Homes: The Relationship between Patient Mix and Nursing Staff Usage." Paper submitted in partial fulfillment of the requirements of the degree of Master of Arts in Public Affairs, University of Minnesota, 1982.

Manard, Barbara. "The Final Injustice: Inequality, Social Welfare, and Old-Age Institutions." Ph.D. dissertation, University of Virginia, 1976.

Manard, Barbara, Cary Kent, and Dirk Van Gils. *Old-Age Institutions.* Lexington, Mass.: D. C. Heath and Company, 1975.

Manard, Barbara, Ralph Woehle, and James Heilman. *Better Homes for the Old.* Lexington, Mass.: D. C. Heath and Company, 1977.

Meiners, Mark. *The Case for Long-Term Care Insurance.* National Center for Health Services Research reprint 1983-381-787:316.

―――. "The Case for Long-Term Care Insurance." *Health Affairs* 2 (Summer 1983).

―――. "Private Coverage of Services Not Covered by Medicare: The Case for Long-Term Care Insurance." Paper presented at the 110th Annual Meeting of the American Public Health Association, November 14–18, 1982, Montreal, Quebec.

―――. "Shifting the Burden: The Potential Role of the Private Sector in Long Term Care Insurance for the Elderly." *American Health Care Association Journal* (March 1982):20–22.

Mendelson, Mary A. *Tender Loving Greed: How the Incredibly Lucrative Nursing Home "Industry" Is Exploiting America's Old People and Defrauding Us All.* New York: Vintage Books, 1979.

Moloney, Thomas W. *What's Being Done about Medicaid?* A Commonwealth Fund Paper. New York: Commonwealth Fund, 1982.

Moss, Frank E., and Val J. Halamandaris. *Too Old, Too Sick, Too Bad.* Germantown, Md.: Aspen Systems Corporation, 1977.

National Center for Health Services Research. *Effects and Costs of Day Care and Homemaker Services for the Chronically Ill: A Randomized Experiment.* DHEW Publication no. PHS 79-3250, 1979.

Pollack, William. "Long Term Care Facility Reimbursement." In John

Holahan et al., *Altering Medicaid Provider Reimbursement Methods.* Washington, D.C.: Urban Institute, 1977.

Shortell, Stephen, and James P. LoGerfo. "Health Services Research and Public Policy: Definitions, Accomplishments, and Potential." *Health Services Research* (Fall 1978):230–38.

Shortell, Stephen, and Marian A. Solomon. "Improving Health Care Policy Research." *Journal of Health Politics, Policy, and Law* 6 (Winter 1982):684–702.

Skinner, Douglas E., and Donald E. Yett. "Estimation of Cost Functions for Health Services: Nursing Home Care." Paper presented at the Fortieth Annual Conference of the Southern Economic Association, November 12, 1970.

Spiegel, Allen D. *Home Health Care: Home Birthing to Hospice Care.* Owings Mills, Md.: National Health Publishing, 1983.

Spitz, Bruce. "Controlling Nursing Home Costs." In *New Approaches to the Medicaid Crisis,* edited by Robert Blendon and Thomas W. Moloney. New York: F & S Press, 1982.

Spitz, Bruce, and June Weeks. "Medicaid Nursing Home Reimbursement in California, Colorado, Connecticut, Illinois, Louisiana, Minnesota, and New York." Working Papers 1216-0 through 1216-6. Washington, D.C.: Urban Institute, 1978–1979.

Steiner, Paula, and Jack Needleman. *Cost Containment in Long Term Care: Options and Issues in State Program Design.* Prepared for the National Center for Health Services Research, 1981.

—————. *Expanding Long Term Care Efforts: Options and Issues in State Program Design.* Prepared for the National Center for Health Services Research, 1981.

Swan, James H., and Charlene Harrington. "Medicaid Reimbursement Systems and Rates for Nursing Homes: Effects on Utilization and Expenditures." Paper presented at the 192d meeting of the American Public Health Care Association, 1984.

Szanton, Peter. *Not Well Advised.* New York: Russell Sage Foundation, 1981.

Toff, Gail. *Alternatives to Institutional Care for the Elderly: An Analysis of State Initiatives.* Washington, D.C.: Intergovernmental Health Policy Project, 1981.

Tynan, Eileen, Daniel Holub, and Robert Schlenker. *A Synthesis of Research on Nursing Home Reimbursement.* Prepared for the National Center for Health Services Research (Contract no. 233-79-3025), 1981.

U.S. Congress. Congressional Budget Office. *Long-Term Care for the Elderly and Disabled.* Budget Issue Paper, February 1977.

U.S. Department of Health and Human Services. Health Care Financing Administration. *Long Term Care: Background and Future Directions,* 1981.

U.S. Department of Health and Human Services. Office of the Assistant Secretary for Planning and Evaluation. *Working Papers on Long-Term Care*, 1981.

Vladeck, Bruce C. *Unloving Care: The Nursing Home Tragedy.* New York: Basic Books, 1980.

Vogel, Ronald, and Hans Palmer, eds. *Long-Term Care: Perspectives from Research and Demonstrations*. U.S. Department of Health and Human Services, Health Care Financing Administration, 19830-391-955, 1983.

Weiss, Carol. *Using Social Research for Public Policy Making*. Lexington, Mass.: D. C. Heath and Company, 1977.

Weiss, Carol, and M. J. Bucuvalas. "Truth Tests and Utility Tests: Decision Makers' Frames of Reference for Social Science Research." *American Sociological Review* 45 (April 1980):302–13.

Weissert, William. "Toward a Continuum of Care for the Elderly: A Note of Caution." *Public Policy* 29 (Summer 1981).

Weissert, William G., Thomas T. H. Wan, and Barbara Livieratos. *Effects and Costs of Day Care and Homemaker Services for the Chronically Ill: A Randomized Experiment*. DHEW Publication no. PHS 79-3258, 1980.

Williams, J. F. "Appropriate Placement of the Chronically Ill and Aged: A Successful Approach by Evaluation." *Journal of the American Medical Association* 266 (December 10, 1973):1332–35.

Wolf and Company. *How Medicaid Pays for Long Term Care*. Washington, D.C.: American Health Care Association, 1978.

Yondorf, Barbara, and Ellen Hekman. *Major Health Issues for the States: 1984*. Health Care Cost Containment Paper no. 2. Denver, Colo.: National Conference of State Legislators, January 1984.

Zimmer, James G. "Characteristics of Patients and Care Provided in Health-related and Skilled Nursing Facilities." *Medical Care* 13 (December 1975):992–1010.

SELECTED AEI PUBLICATIONS

Medicaid and Other Experiments in State Health Policy, Rosemary Gibson Kern and Susan R. Windham with Paula Griswold (1986, 74 pp., $4.95)

The Health Policy Agenda: Some Critical Questions, Marion Ein Lewin, ed. (1985, 126 pp., cloth $16.95, paper $8.95)

Evaluating State Medicaid Reforms, Pamela L. Haynes (1985, 36 pp., $4.95)

Incentives vs. Controls in Health Policy: Broadening the Debate, Jack A. Meyer, ed. (1985, 156 pp., cloth $15.95, paper $7.95)

Securing a Safer Blood Supply: Two Views, Ross D. Eckert and Edward L. Wallace (1985, 153 pp., cloth $16.95, paper $8.95)

Medicaid Reform: Four Studies of Case Management, Deborah A. Freund with Polly M. Ehrenhaft and Marie Hackbarth (1984, 83 pp., $5.95)

Managing Health Care Costs: Private Sector Innovations, Sean Sullivan, ed., with Polly M. Ehrenhaft (1984, 106 pp., cloth $15.95, paper $7.95)

• *Mail orders for publications to:* AMERICAN ENTERPRISE INSTITUTE, 1150 Seventeenth Street, N.W., Washington, D.C. 20036 • *For postage and handling, add 10 percent of total; minimum charge $2, maximum $10 (no charge on prepaid orders)* • *For information on orders, or to expedite service, call toll free 800-424-2873 (in Washington, D.C., 202-862-5869)* • *Prices subject to change without notice* • *Payable in U.S. currency through U.S. banks only*

AEI ASSOCIATES PROGRAM

The American Enterprise Institute invites your participation in the competition of ideas through its AEI Associates Program. This program has two objectives: (1) to extend public familiarity with contemporary issues; and (2) to increase research on these issues and disseminate the results to policy makers, the academic community, journalists, and others who help shape public policies. The areas studied by AEI include Economic Policy, International Policy, and Political and Social Processes. For the $49 annual fee, Associates receive
  • a subscription to *Memorandum,* the newsletter on all AEI activities
  • the AEI publications catalog and all supplements
  • a 30 percent discount on all AEI books
  • a 40 percent discount for certain seminars on key issues
  • subscriptions to the following publications: *Public Opinion,* a bi-monthly magazine exploring trends and implications of public opinion on social and public policy questions; and the *AEI Economist,* a monthly newsletter analyzing current economic issues and evaluating future trends.

Call 202/862-7170 or write: AMERICAN ENTERPRISE INSTITUTE
1150 Seventeenth Street, N.W., Suite 301, Washington, D.C. 20036

"The work of the authors presented in this volume constitutes a significant step in improving our understanding of how research can be more effectively brought to bear on important policy questions."

From the Foreword by ROBERT J. BLENDON
Senior Vice President
The Robert Wood Johnson Foundation

From Research into Policy

Improving the Link for Health Services

MARION EIN LEWIN, editor

How does health services research become health policy? What is the role of such research in controlling health care costs? in developing prospective payment systems for hospitals? in helping states to respond to federal cutbacks? in reforming the reimbursement of nursing homes? This book addresses these questions, in the following chapters:

LYNN ETHEREDGE, *Government and Health Care Costs: The Influence of Research on Policy*

JOEL MENGES, *From Health Services Research to Federal Law: The Case of DRGs*

IRA MOSCOVICE, *Health Services Research and the Policymaking Process: State Response to Federal Cutbacks in Programs Affecting Child Health*

BARBARA BOLLING MANARD, *Doing Research for Decision Makers: Nursing Home Reimbursement*

MARION EIN LEWIN is director of the Center for Health Policy Research at the American Enterprise Institute. She is the editor of *The Health Policy Agenda: Some Critical Questions* (AEI, 1985).

 American Enterprise Institute for Public Policy Research
1150 Seventeenth Street, N.W., Washington, D.C. 20036

ISBN 0-8447-3605-8